THE SERIES

AUTHENTIC MANHOOD — VOLUME **5** TRAINING GUIDE

A **MAN** AND HIS **MARRIAGE**

D1529292

authenticmanhood.com

A **MAN** AND HIS **MARRIAGE**

Published by Authentic Manhood
Copyright 2014 Fellowship Associates Inc.
First printing 2014

ISBN 978-1-4300-3202-1
Item 005644085

Project Management & Art Direction: Rachel Lindholm
Design: Samantha Corcoran, Mike Robinson, Details Communications, Lindsey Woodward
Editors: Rick Caldwell, Grant Edwards, Rachel Lindholm, Katie Ryburn, Steve Snider, Rebekah Wallace, Lindsey Woodward
Contributors: Mike Boschetti, Rick Caldwell, Brian Goins, Sheila Wray Gregoire, Tierce Green, Toby Kurth, Steve Snider, Paul Tripp, Zac Allen
Authentic Manhood, Men's Fraternity, and 33 The Series are registered trademarks of Fellowship Associates Inc.

To order additional copies of this resource, go to **authenticmanhood.com**

Printed in the United States of America

Distributed by:

Authentic Manhood
12115 Hinson Road, Suite 200
Little Rock, AR 72112

Adult Ministry Publishing
LifeWay Church Resources
One LifeWay Plaza
Nashville, TN 37234-0152

TABLE CONTENTS

How to **Experience 33** as an **Individual** or a **Group**

33 The Series can be viewed on DVD, downloaded from *authenticmanhood.com*, or experienced via mobile apps. Any of these three delivery systems can be utilized by groups or individuals. *One of the great things about this series is the variety of ways it can be used and/or presented.*

The series is organized in a way that provides flexibility and offers a variety of options on how the material can be experienced. *33* is organized into six topically themed volumes that include six sessions each. *Volumes include topics on a man's design, story, traps, parenting, marriage, and career.* You can choose to commit to one volume/topic at a time, limit a particular experience to six sessions, or combine multiple volumes into one expanded experience that includes more sessions (12, 18, 24, 30, or 36). You can also choose any combination of these options.

However you choose to experience 33, the manhood principles and practical insights taught in each volume are essential for every man on the journey to Authentic Manhood. 33

How to Make the Most of **Your** 33 **Experience**

33 **The Series** *is more than just a video series for you to watch and then mark off your list. When experienced with other men, it can be the pathway to Authentic Manhood that changes your life forever. Authentic Manhood is truly a movement that you can become a part of and then passionately invite others to join.*

1 Make sure you have a team. Your experience will be greatly enhanced if you form a team with other men or at least one other man to help process the truths you receive.

2 Make sure every man has a 33 Training Guide. A 33 Training Guide will enable men to take notes, record a strategic move after each session, and create an action plan at the end. It also contains articles, interviews, and features that will support the truths men receive from the video teaching.

3 Make sure you stay caught up. All the sessions of 33 can be purchased online and downloaded for only a few dollars per session. If you are viewing 33 with a group and miss a session, you can download the session you missed and stay caught up. (Purchase downloads at *www.authenticmanhood.com.*)

Most importantly...

4 Make sure you pass on the truths you learn to other men. When session six ends, the exciting part just begins. Don't just sit back and wait for another study. Instead, step up and find another man or group of men to lead through the volume you just completed. For a small investment of just a few dollars, you can download your very own set of this series and use it to make a HUGE investment in the lives of other men.

PLAY

33 is a resource that can set you up to influence the lives of other men tremendously.

Going through **33** yourself should be only the beginning.

Here's your challenge to PLAY BIG:

After you complete this volume, download the videos at
AUTHENTICMANHOOD.com
for just a few dollars
and take another man or group of men through the series.

BIG

REJECT PASSIVITY
ACCEPT RESPONSIBILITY
LEAD COURAGEOUSLY
INVEST ETERNALLY

LIVE IT OUT!

The Presenters

BRYAN CARTER

Bryan Carter taught the original Men's Fraternity curriculum to a group of more than eight hundred men over a three-year period at Concord Church. Additionally, he has been a frequent speaker at local and international churches, conferences, and events.

Bryan is the senior pastor of Concord Church in Dallas, Texas.

He is the author of a 28-day devotional book titled *Great Expectations*. Bryan also contributed to the book *What Two White Men of God Learned from Black Men of God,* coauthored by Dr. Joel Gregory and Dr. Bill Crouch.

A recreational basketball player, Bryan is a fan of the NBA's Dallas Mavericks.

Bryan and his wife, Stephanie, are the parents of two daughters, Kaitlyn and Kennedy, and one son, Carson.

TIERCE GREEN

Tierce Green is the pastor of House Churches at Church Project in The Woodlands, Texas, where his primary role is to call men up and equip them to lead and care for people. He also travels extensively as a speaker at conferences and training events. He taught the principles of Authentic Manhood to more than a thousand men each week over a seven-year period in a seasonal gathering called The Quest.

Tierce created and produced a 12-session video series for men called *Fight Club: Some Things Are Worth Fighting For.* He has also written curriculum for Student Life and LifeWay.

Tierce is a lifelong Dallas Cowboys fan. His favorite activities include landscaping, grilling just about anything, and having good conversations.

Tierce and his wife, Dana, were married in 1987. They have one daughter, Anna.

JOHN BRYSON

Seeing firsthand the impact the original Men's Fraternity curriculum had on his own life, John Bryson decided to teach the material himself. In the years since, he has led thousands of men through the basic ideas of biblical manhood.

John is a cofounding teaching pastor of Fellowship Memphis in Memphis, Tennessee.

In 2010 he completed his doctor of ministry from Gordon-Conwell Theological Seminary. John is also the author of *College Ready,* a curriculum for college students, and travels the country consulting and investing in churches, church planters, leaders, and new ideas.

A native of Harlan, Kentucky, John played baseball at Asbury College.

John and his wife, Beth, have six children: Brooke, Beck, Bo, Boss, Blair, and Bayne.

Foundation

SESSION **ONE** | Training Guide

**My name is Paul Trip.
I don't know you, but I do know that
there is hope for your marriage.**

NOT a hopeless marriage

Your marriage has hope but not because of how compatible you and your spouse are. Your marriage has hope but not because of how much money you have. Your marriage has hope but not because of how often you go to church and read the Bible.

Your marriage has hope because of the person and work of Jesus Christ.

I DON'T KNOW IF YOU'RE single, engaged, happily married, angrily married, somewhere in between, divorced or widowed. I don't know if your parents had a healthy marriage, if their marriage was plagued by selfish decisions, or if your parents were even married.

I don't know about the quality of your marriage. Maybe you have grown in love and affection for your spouse and you would say that you love each other more than ever. Maybe the person you once adored has become an object of your irritation; the romantic spark died long ago, and you simply cohabitate with the person featured in your wedding album.

I don't know about your experience with marriage, but there is one thing I know: regardless of who you are, where you live, or whom you're married to, your marriage has hope.

The apostle Paul says, "The love of Christ controls us, because we have concluded this: that one has died for all, therefore all have died; and he died for all, that those who live might no longer live for themselves but for him who for their sake died and was raised" (2 Cor. 5:14-15, ESV).

I'm about to hurt your feelings, but it's crucial that you understand this: you are your biggest marriage problem. The previous Bible verse says you live for yourself. That's another way of saying you're selfish.

You bring that selfishness into your marriage; the Bible calls it sin. Your sin will erode and ultimately destroy your marriage. You won't love your spouse; you'll love yourself. You won't desire what's best for your marriage; you'll desire what's most pleasurable for you in that moment.

Jesus refuses to tolerate sin in a marriage. But instead of lashing out in anger and punishing you, Jesus took the punishment you deserve and satisfied the just wrath of God. He now lives in your marriage by His Spirit and works every day to free you from selfishness. Because Jesus died to free you from sin, your marriage has more hope than it ever had before. You are now freed to love your spouse sacrificially; you are now freed to say no to selfish desires; you are now freed to chase after God's will in your marriage.

BECAUSE JESUS DIED TO FREE YOU FROM SIN,

your marriage has more hope than it ever had before. You are now freed to love your spouse sacrificially; you are now freed to say no to selfish desires; you are now freed to chase after God's will in your marriage.

This freedom was earned all at once on the cross, but your freedom won't be complete overnight. Change is rarely an event; change is almost always a process. You'll need to work at loving your spouse sacrificially. You'll need to work at saying no to selfish desires. You'll need to work at chasing after God's will in your marriage.

This curriculum will help you understand and pursue your freedom in Christ, but you need to prepare your heart. I encourage you to prepare in <u>three</u> ways.

1. Prepare to Fire Your Inner Lawyer

This curriculum will expose your sin. Because evidence of your selfishness will be exhibited, you'll be tempted to hire an inner lawyer who argues for your righteousness. Your lawyer will try to persuade you that your sin isn't as bad as that of others and your spouse is the ultimate problem. Fire this lawyer right now.

<u>If you duck the conviction of the Holy Spirit and point the finger of blame to your spouse, you will slow the progress of change because you don't think you need to change.</u>

Jesus died for each and every one of your sins. That means you don't have to be afraid of having that sin exposed. Put down your defense and admit that you're as sinful as the Bible says.

2. Prepare to Run to Jesus

When your sin has been exposed and your inner lawyer has been fired, there's only one thing to do: run to Jesus. He has already forgiven all your sin, and He now walks with you every step of the way as you struggle with sin and search for freedom in this life.

------------------------------ ◆ ------------------------------

Only Jesus has the ability to change your heart and change your marriage.

------------------------------ ◆ ------------------------------

When you're facing the reality of your selfishness and struggling in your marriage, cry out for help and run to Jesus. He wants nothing more than for His people to come running, broken and humble, for help.

3. Prepare to Help Others

God might place you next to someone who needs marriage help, and He might choose you to be that instrument of grace in their marriage.

This curriculum offers a great opportunity for you to receive grace. You will learn from people who have studied the Bible for decades and who have counseled hundreds of marriages. The questions will ask you to examine your heart with honesty. Take full advantage of grace.

But it's important to recognize that God doesn't call you to be only a recipient of grace; He calls you to participate in the work of grace as well.

Have a soft and compassionate heart for those who are hurting. Be prepared to listen and to speak truth in love to those who need it. You don't need to be a professional counselor or a licensed pastor to minister to other Christians.

Foundation Presented by Bryan Carter

I. INTRODUCTION

1. Too many of us are _____ in our marriages.

2. Marriage is about way more than just your _____ _____ and positive outcomes on society.

II. THE DIVINE ORIGIN OF MARRIAGE

1. Genesis 2:18-25 (ESV) "The LORD God said, 'It is not good that the man should be alone; I will make him a helper fit for him.' ... So the LORD God caused a deep sleep to fall upon the man, and while he slept took one of his ribs and closed up its place with flesh. And the rib that the LORD God had taken from the man he made into a woman and brought her to the man. Then the man said, 'This at last is bone of my bones and flesh of my flesh; she shall be called Woman, because she was taken out of Man.' Therefore a man shall leave his father and his mother and hold fast to his wife, and they shall become one flesh. And the man and his wife were both naked and were not ashamed."

2. Four foundational truths this passage teaches us about marriage:

- Marriage was _____ idea.

  o One man with one woman in a unique covenant relationship.

- God said that it was not good for man to be _____.

- God created a _____ suitable for man.

  o The woman was created to co-rule the earth with the man, not to be ruled by him.

- God intended man to leave his parents' home and to _____ to his wife.

  o The word "cling" carries with it the idea of maintaining a covenant relationship.[1]

  o God didn't intend marriage as a _____ arrangement.

III. GOD'S DESIGN FOR MARRIAGE

1. Throughout history there have generally been three different approaches to marriage:

- The "_____" marriage

  o In this type of marriage, it can feel like there are a winner and a loser.

- The "_____" marriage

  o The identical marriage is an overcorrection for the top-down marriage.

- The "_____" Biblical marriage

  o Emphasizes equality and fairness but also leaves room for leadership and God's intended differences between a husband and wife.

2. God's vision and design for a Biblical marriage in Ephesians 5:22-33 (ESV):

"Wives, submit to your own husbands, as to the Lord. For the husband is the head of the wife even as Christ is the head of the church, his body, and is himself its Savior. Now as the church submits to Christ, so also wives should submit in everything to their husbands.

Husbands, love your wives, as Christ loved the church and gave himself up for her. ... Husbands should love their wives as their own bodies. He who loves his wife loves himself. ... Let each one of you love his wife as himself, and let the wife see that she respects her husband."

1. Victor P. Hamilton, *The Book of Genesis, Chapters 1–17*, New International Commentary on the Old Testament (Grand Rapids: Eerdmans, 1990), 181.

SESSION ONE | FOUNDATION

3. Husband's Biblical role: "Headship" is the husband's divinely appointed role to provide responsible
_____ _____ in his home.[2]

  • Headship is a divine appointment.

  • Leadership means you take the initiative and the responsibility for key aspects of your marriage and family.

  • The key word in our definition of headship is the word _____.

    o Being a servant leader means that, like Jesus, you are others-centered.

    o All healthy marriages are built on and around _____.

4. Wife's Biblical role: "Submission" is the wife's divinely appointed role to use her gifts and attitude to affirm her husband's leadership and initiative.

  • Submission does not mean a "_____" person.

  • Submission is not something a man demands from his wife.

  • Submission does not mean an enabler of wrongdoing; it only means empowering of right-doing.

2. This definition is drawn primarily from Robert Lewis, "A Man and His Wife, Parts 1 & 2," in *The Quest for Authentic Manhood* (Nashville: LifeWay, 2003). Our definitions of *headship* and *submission* were also influenced by John Piper, *This Momentary Marriage* (Wheaton, IL: Crossway, 2009), 80, and George W. Knight III, "Husbands and Wives as Analogues of Christ and the Church," in *Recovering Biblical Manhood and Womanhood*, ed. John Piper and Wayne Grudem (Wheaton, IL: Crossway, 2006), 165–78.

Be sure to check out Paul Tripp's great marriage resources at paultripp.com and on Twitter @PaulTripp.

DISCUSSION / REFLECTION QUESTIONS

1. At the beginning of the session, Bryan mentioned that many men often feel "stuck" or "numb" in their marriage. Are there aspects of your marriage where you feel "stuck" or "numb"?

2. How does the fact that marriage was God's idea impact our approach to it?

3. Why do you think the "identical marriage" has been embraced by most of Western culture? Why do you think "submission" gets such a bad rap in modern society? How can husbands abuse their role of "headship"?

4. Bryan said "grace" is foundational in marriage and should be at the core of a husband's leadership. What does it look like for "grace" to be at the core of your marriage and leadership?

AUTHENTIC MANHOOD

YOUR **STRATEGIC MOVE**

RESOURCES ON THE FOLLOWING PAGES

- Naked and Unashamed (p. 20–23)

- The 4 Foundational Truths (p. 24–25)

- **THE RED ZONE**: Marriage Statistics (p. 26–27)

NAKED & UNASHAMED

"LOVE US." HEARING THOSE TWO WORDS UNDID ME. I WAS WATCHING "MY LIFE," A MOVIE ABOUT A GUY NAMED BOB JONES (PLAYED BY MICHAEL KEATON) WHO IS DYING FROM CANCER.

At one point Bob's pregnant wife, Gail (played by Nicole Kidman), discovers that Bob has secretly made a series of home movies that will teach his yet-to-be-born son about life. The videos have a real "life is tough so you have to be tough" tone. And Gail is furious after seeing the videos. But I didn't understand why. As I watched the movie, I was thinking, Give the

guy a break. He's dying. And then she says those two words: "Love us." Finally, I realized what was really going on. Bob was dying—he was experiencing great physical and emotional pain—and he was keeping his wife out of it. Gail was begging him to love her by letting her in on what he was feeling. And then the scales fell off my own eyes.

I watched this movie for the first time at a men's retreat in the Ozark Mountains. I had only recently come out of the fog I had lived in for over a decade. On the outside, it seemed I had it all together. But on the inside, I was a mess.

I was isolated, prone to binge drinking, had engaged in multiple affairs, and struggled with pornography. I walked out on my first marriage and my second marriage was now coming to an end. All before I was 35 years old. But in the middle of the devastation, I

already had reason to have hope. God graciously sent his Spirit into my heart, bringing me from death to new life. The retreat was an opportunity for me and some other men to wrestle with our very screwed-up notions as to what it meant to be a man.

After watching that movie, I realized that no one in my life knew if I really loved them. How could they? I spent most of my adult life keeping secrets and working as hard as I could to manage my image. I did not share my feelings with anyone, especially the women I had been married to. Not surprisingly, I was completely oblivious to the love others had for me. In other words, I was clueless as to how to give or receive love.

Feeling isolated from the love of God and the love of others fueled my destructive sin habits.

Fundamentally, my isolation and lack of emotional intimacy were rooted in my sin, especially my pride. We tend to think of a prideful person as someone who is vain or makes much of his own accomplishments. While a man like that is definitely prideful, it is not the only way one can struggle with pride. Pride is self-centeredness of any type. For some, it may be the conceited type of pride just mentioned. But pride can also be present in the context of a condemning and shameful view of self. The arrogant person and the person weighed down by shame, seemingly opposites, share this in common: self-centeredness is their grid for interpreting life and relationships.

Before sin came into the garden, the affections of Adam were pointed toward God; he was able to worship God with all his heart, soul, mind, and strength. But God had created man in His image, and to enjoy intimate community with Him and his wife. God said it was not good for man to be alone (see Gen. 2:18). So God created a woman to whom man would "hold fast" (Gen. 2:24, ESV) in a lifelong covenantal relationship. The joining of their flesh physically (both in the creation of Eve from Adam's rib and in their sexual union) points to emotional and spiritual intimacy that allowed them to be naked and unashamed with one another and with God (see Gen. 2:25). Because there was no sin in Adam or Eve, there was no self-centeredness.

Then it all changed in Genesis 3:6, when Adam and Eve bought into the lie of Satan, daring to believe they could be like God, and ate the forbidden fruit. With their sin came shame (the first consequence of sin) and alienation from God and one another. Martin Luther said that because of the fall, our human nature has now become self-centered. Instead of our affections naturally drawing us toward God and toward our spouses, they instead point back to us. [1]

OUR NATURAL TENDENCY IS NOW TO FOCUS ON OURSELVES, TO BE SELF-OBSESSED, SECRETIVE, & FEARFUL.

Instead of wanting to share what is inside us with our wives so that they can be the helpmate God designed them to be, now in our sin we see intimacy as dangerous to us, creating fear of exposure or loss of control. Tim Keller calls this self-centered approach to marriage a cancer that is the root cause of divorce. Self-centeredness in one spouse (who is usually blind to it) provokes self-centeredness in the other spouse, resulting in a "downward spiral into self-pity, anger, and despair, as the relationship gets eaten away to nothing." [2]

1. Martin Luther (1972-06-01). Luther's Works, vol. 25, Lectures on Romans (Kindle edition) (Saint Louis: Concordia), Kindle locations 7850–51.

2. Timothy Keller (2011-11-01). The Meaning of Marriage: Facing the Complexities of Commitment with the Wisdom of God (Kindle edition) (New York: Penguin), 48–49.

I actively practiced self-centeredness in my marriage in two big ways. First, I withheld sharing my struggles and needs out of fear of rejection (shame) and a mistaken belief that I truly did not need the care of others, especially my wife. My self-centeredness told me I was being self-sufficient and not a burden—almost an admirable quality, right? (Wrong!) Second, I was self-centered by covering up my sin rather than embracing God's prescription of confession and repentance. By not owning up to my sin, I thought I could avoid painful consequences and, sadly, even keep engaging in my sin. I had warped any sense of intimacy into illicit sex. I was trapped in a prison of self—by me, for me.

SO HOW DO WE REGAIN THE INTIMACY FOR WHICH GOD DESIGNED US? SINCE THE SELF-CENTEREDNESS THAT KILLS MARRIAGES IS ROOTED IN THE FALL, THEN OUR ONLY HOPE FOR RESTORING INTIMACY MUST COME FROM THE GOSPEL.

Intimacy existed between man and God before it did between man and woman and our loss of spiritual intimacy with God is the biggest hurdle we face. A holy God will not draw near to us as long as we remain alienated from Him by our sin (see Eph. 2:14). We are dead in our trespasses (see Col. 2:13), and a dead person cannot do anything to save himself. On our own we are without hope of ever experiencing true intimacy with Him again. But God, because of His rich mercy and great love for us (see Eph. 2:4), took the initiative to reconcile us to Himself through the cross of Jesus Christ.

By our faith in the atoning work of Christ, we have received grace upon grace. Our debt to God for our sin has been placed on Christ, and His perfect righteousness has been credited to us (see 2 Cor. 5:21). For those who believe the gospel, intimacy with God has now been restored. Our intimacy with Him is even deeper now than it was in the garden. God's intimate love for us has now been poured into our hearts because His Spirit has actually taken up residence there (see Rom. 5:5). God is now inside us. What could be more intimate than that?

SO HOW DOES INTIMACY WITH GOD—NOW RESTORED THROUGH THE GOSPEL—OVERCOME OUR TENDENCY TO BE SELF-CENTERED?

1 First, because the penalty of our sin has been paid for by Christ, we are freed from the condemnation we justly deserve for our sin. Our sin has now been covered over. What a puny fig leaf could not do, the blood of Christ flowing on the cross was more than sufficient to do. Keeping secrets kills intimacy. And because Jesus became our sin and took on the shame of that sin, we can come out of the bushes because there's no need to hide anymore. That restores intimacy with those we love.

2 Second, in Christ we have been made new (see 2 Cor. 5:17). We have a new identity in Christ that has secured for us an heirship that is guaranteed by the Holy Spirit (see Eph. 1:11-14). Because what Christ has given us is so much more than the identities we try to create for ourselves, we can let go of the petty self-centeredness that seeks to build ourselves up and rob us of intimacy with our spouse when they challenge our self-made image.

TULLIAN TCHIVIDJIAN DESCRIBES IT THIS WAY:

BECAUSE JESUS WON FOR YOU, YOU'RE FREE TO LOSE. BECAUSE JESUS WAS SOMEONE, YOU'RE FREE TO BE NO ONE. BECAUSE JESUS WAS EXTRAORDINARY, YOU'RE FREE TO BE ORDINARY. BECAUSE JESUS SUCCEEDED FOR YOU, YOU'RE FREE TO FAIL.[3]

I would add to that, we are finally free to be known. That freedom restores intimacy with our spouses and allows us to once again be naked and unashamed (see Gen. 2:25).

So, how does intimacy secured by the gospel work itself out on the ground in our homes and marriages? First, we have to remember that because we are simultaneously saint (because of grace) and sinner (because of still indwelling sin), we desire intimacy with God and our spouse, yet, at the same time, still struggle with self-centeredness. That tension is the fight of faith we engage in every day: to believe the promises of the gospel (see John 6:29) and to reject our self-centered ways that seek to isolate us from the love of God and our wives. So we must constantly look at ourselves and make sure what we believe is in keeping with the gospel (see 2 Cor. 13:5).

Second, an implication of our faith in the gospel is that we stand in an all-sufficient grace that empowers us to live in keeping with that gospel. In our flesh, we will not want to be open and vulnerable with our spouse, so effort alone will not get us where we want to be.

GRACE MUST DO IT FOR US. EVERY DAY WE EMBRACE GOD'S ORDAINED MEANS OF GRACE, SUCH AS STUDYING SCRIPTURE, PRAYER, AND PRACTICING OTHER DISCIPLINES OF THE FAITH, TO TRAIN OURSELVES AND TO BRING OUR SINFUL FLESH UNDER THE CONTROL OF GOD'S SPIRIT.

Finally, we must begin to trust our wives with ourselves. As Paul Tripp says, you must "place [4] yourself in ... her care." Let her love you by trusting her to be the helpmate God has designed her to be. She is His provision for you. To do that, she needs to know what you need, what you fear, what delights you. Simply put, she needs to know you. Ask for God's grace every day to share yourself with her. Share your wins and losses for the day. Even share your sin. And when you open up to receiving her love by trusting her with you, she in turn will feel loved.

That is knowing and being known. That is the opposite of self-centeredness. That is intimacy.

[3] Tullian Tchividjian, One-Way Love: Inexhaustible Grace for an Exhausted World (Colorado Springs: David C. Cook, 2013), 36.

[4] Paul David Tripp, What Did You Expect? Redeeming the Realities of Marriage (Wheaton, IL: Crossway, 2010), 149.

TRUTH

1

Marriage was God's idea.

❯ God defined marriage as between one man and one woman.

❯ We don't take our cues from society or culture but from the original Designer.

TRUTH

2

God said it's not good for man to be alone.

❯ God knew man would function better with a partner.

❯ When it comes to physical, emotional, spiritual, and sexual well-being, men are at their best in marriage.

4 FOUNDATIONAL TRUTHS ABOUT MARRIAGE

TRUTH 3

God created a helper suitable for man.

> She is not only a companion who complements and helps him but also someone for him to love, serve, and enjoy.

> The differences between men and women aren't accidental; they're intentionally designed with our best in mind.

TRUTH 4

God intended a man to leave his parents' home and cling to his wife.

> A man is to leave the dependence of his parents' home and to create his own self-sustaining family unit.

> A man is to become attached to his wife in a unique covenant relationship and bond with her physically, emotionally, and spiritually in a way he experiences with no one else.

MARRIAGE STATISTICS

78%

SEVENTY-EIGHT PERCENT [1]

OF AMERICAN ADULTS ARE MARRIED

33%

THIRTY-THREE PERCENT

OF AMERICANS HAVE BEEN DIVORCED

84%

EIGHTY-FOUR PERCENT [1]

OF BORN-AGAIN CHRISTIANS ARE MARRIED

29

TWENTY-NINE YEARS [2]

IS THE AVERAGE AGE WHEN MEN GET MARRIED

73%

SEVENTY-THREE PERCENT [3]

OF DIVORCED COUPLES SAID LACK OF COMMITMENT WAS THE REASON FOR SPLITTING UP

56%

FIFTY-SIX PERCENT [4]

OF DIVORCE CASES INVOLVED ONE PARTY HAVING AN OBSESSIVE INTEREST IN PORNOGRAPHIC WEBSITES

70%

SEVENTY PERCENT [5]

OF MARRIED COUPLES SAY THE DETERMINING FACTOR IN WHETHER THEY FEEL SATISFIED WITH SEX, ROMANCE, AND PASSION IS THE QUALITY OF THEIR FRIENDSHIP WITH EACH OTHER

FOOTNOTES

1 https://www.barna.org/barna-update/article/15-familykids/42-new-marriage-and-divorce-statistics-released#.U-PX6RZhTA4

2 http://www.huffingtonpost.com/2014/05/14/reasons-not-to-get-married_n_5274911.html

3 http://living.msn.com/love-relationships/the-8-most-common-reasons-for-divorce#9

4 http://www.covenanteyes.com/pornstats/

5 http://lifehacker.com/this-infographic-reveals-the-secrets-of-the-happiest-co-1518305669

SESSION ONE | FOUNDATION

SCRIPTURE REFERENCES

Genesis 1:28 (ESV) "God blessed them. And God said to them, 'Be fruitful and multiply and fill the earth and subdue it, and have dominion over the fish of the sea and over the birds of the heavens and over every living thing that moves on the earth.'"

Genesis 2:18-25 (ESV) "The LORD God said, 'It is not good that the man should be alone; I will make him a helper fit for him.' ... So the LORD God caused a deep sleep to fall upon the man, and while he slept took one of his ribs and closed up its place with flesh. And the rib that the LORD God had taken from the man he made into a woman and brought her to the man. Then the man said, 'This at last is bone of my bones and flesh of my flesh; she shall be called Woman, because she was taken out of Man.' Therefore a man shall leave his father and his mother and hold fast to his wife, and they shall become one flesh. And the man and his wife were both naked and were not ashamed."

Ephesians 5:22-33 (ESV) "Wives, submit to your own husbands, as to the Lord. For the husband is the head of the wife even as Christ is the head of the church, his body, and is himself its Savior. Now as the church submits to Christ, so also wives should submit in everything to their husbands. Husbands, love your wives, as Christ loved the church and gave himself up for her. ... Husbands should love their wives as their own bodies. He who loves his wife loves himself. ... Let each one of you love his wife as himself, and let the wife see that she respects her husband."

SUPPORTING RESOURCES

Knight, George W., III. *"Husbands and Wives as Analogues of Christ and the Church: Ephesians 5:21-33 and Colossians 3:18-19."* In *Recovering Biblical Manhood and Womanhood,* edited by John Piper and Wayne Grudem, 165–78. Wheaton, IL: Crossway, 2006. A scholarly and exegetical analysis of Ephesians 5:21-33.

Ortlund, Raymond C., Jr. *"Male-Female Equality and Male Headship: Genesis 1-3."* In *Recovering Biblical Manhood and Womanhood,* edited by John Piper and Wayne Grudem, 95–112. Wheaton, IL: Crossway, 2006. A scholarly and exegetical analysis of Genesis 1-3.

Piper, John. *This Momentary Marriage: A Parable of Permanence.* Wheaton, IL: Crossway, 2009. Pastor and theologian John Piper discusses a Biblical vision for marriage, relying heavily on Genesis 1-3 and Ephesians 5.

The content in the previous resources does not necessarily reflect the opinion of Authentic Manhood. Readers should utilize these resources but form their own opinions.

Die to Live

SESSION **TWO** | Training Guide

SESSION TWO | DIE TO LIVE

Die to Live Presented by Tierce Green

I. INTRODUCTION

1. The enemy to servant leadership is _____.

2. Philippians 2:3 (ESV) Paul reminds us to "do nothing from selfish ambition or conceit, but in humility count others more significant than yourselves."

II. THE ENEMY OF SERVANT LEADERSHIP: YOU

1. A game-changing statement: marriage isn't primarily about our

   _____.

2. Authentic Manhood is about a life that is lived for God and for others.

3. Matthew 22:37-39 (ESV) "... love the Lord your God with all your heart and with all your soul and with all your mind. This is the great and first commandment. And a second is like it: You shall love your neighbor as yourself."

4. When you are focused on yourself and your own happiness ... _____ are your biggest enemy to servant leadership.

III. THE ESSENCE OF SERVANT LEADERSHIP

1. The "Paradox Principle": we die to ourselves in order to truly live. We _____ to live.

- In Luke 9:23-24 (ESV) Jesus told His followers: "If anyone would come after me, let him deny himself and take up his cross daily and follow me. For whoever would save his life will lose it, but whoever loses his life for my sake will save it."

- In Mark 10:43-45 (ESV) Jesus said: "... whoever would be great among you must be your servant, ... for even the Son of Man came not to be served but to serve, and to give his life as a ransom for many."

- In Philippians 2:4-7 (ESV) the Apostle Paul said this about Jesus: "Let each of you look not only to his own interests, but also to the interests of others. Have this mind among yourselves, which is yours in Christ Jesus, who, though he was in the form of God, did not count equality with God a thing to be grasped, but emptied himself, by taking the form of a servant."

2. The grace Jesus offers us in His self-sacrifice is both the _____ and the _____ for our servant leadership in marriage.

- Our example: Ephesians 5:25 (ESV) says, "Husbands, love your wives, as Christ loved the church and gave himself up for her."

- Our motivation: When we have personally experienced God's amazing grace toward us and the power of His forgiveness in our own life, we become motivated and even _____ to forgive and show that same grace to our wife.

  o Colossians 3:13 (ESV) "... as the Lord has forgiven you, so you also must forgive."

3. The "Paradox Principle" is at the core of every _____ and vibrant marriage.

SESSION TWO | DIE TO LIVE

IV. THE DIFFERENT AREAS OF SERVANT LEADERSHIP

- **As Servant Leader, the husband is called to be the:**

  - Spiritual Leader

  - Emotional Encourager

  - Financial Provider

  - Physical Protector

1. The husband's role as spiritual leader:

   - This doesn't mean you have to be some spiritual _____.

   - As we bless the soul of our wife, our soul is blessed as well.

2. The husband's role as emotional encourager:

   - This is all about being aware of and sensitive to our wife's _____.

   - 1 Peter 3:7 (ESV) tells husbands to "... live with your wives in an understanding way."

   - Wise is the husband who makes a habit of keeping up to date and being keenly aware of what his wife is _____ and thinking.

   - Wise is the husband who does the work to know himself emotionally.

- This includes the oversight of joy and _____ in your home.

3. The husband's role as financial provider:

- Financial provision for the home is a basic _____ of manhood.

- 1 Timothy 5:8 (ESV) "If anyone does not provide for his relatives, and especially for members of his household, he has denied the faith and is worse than an unbeliever."

- Oversight of the financial health also means you're planning for the _____.

4. The husband's role as physical protector:

- At a very basic level, this means a husband stands between his family and physical danger.

- He takes the lead and supports his wife by staying on top of what his family is _____ from the outside, proactively guiding them toward healthy influences.

Be sure to check out Paul Tripp's great marriage resources at paultripp.com and on Twitter @PaulTripp.

DISCUSSION / REFLECTION QUESTIONS

1. Pastor Tim Keller says that "if two spouses each say, 'I'm going to treat my self-centeredness as the main problem in the marriage,' you have the prospect of a truly great marriage." Do you agree with this statement? Do you believe that you are your biggest enemy to servant leadership? Discuss.

2. Have you ever experienced the "Paradox Principle" (die to live) in your marriage or in any other aspect of your life? What did it look like?

3. What are some ways you could die to yourself more that would give new life to your marriage?

4. Tierce talked about four important areas for husbands to be a "servant leader": spiritual leader, emotional encourager, financial provider, and physical protector. Which of these comes easiest to you? Where do you need to make some adjustments or get some help?

RESOURCES ON THE FOLLOWING PAGES

- Is Marriage About My Happiness? Or Is It About Something Bigger? (p. 36–37)

- Die to Live (p. 38–39)

- THE RED ZONE: Marriage Is... (p. 40–41)

IS MARRIAGE ABOUT MY HAPPINESS?

OR IS IT ABOUT

SOMETHING BIGGER?

BY TOBY KURTH

WE LIVE IN A TIME IN HISTORY WHEN IT SEEMS THAT HAPPINESS AND PERSONAL FULFILLMENT ARE THE GOALS OF EVERY ENDEAVOR. When people are faced with challenges in life or marriage, the first question they often ask is "What will make you the happiest?" If your job is not bringing you happiness, then quit. If your marriage is not making you happy, then you owe it to yourself to get a divorce. But there is a trap in this thinking that many of us never see: we focus on being happy more than we do on God's design for us. God designed us to live for Him and to live for others. When we are driven merely by happiness and self-fulfillment, we bring destructive behaviors and consequences into our lives and relationships. There is no place this is more true than in marriage.

God wants your marriage relationship to make you and your wife more like Him. **God wants to use your marriage to help make you ... not just happy ... but, more importantly, holy.** As we learn to embrace God's plan for marriage, a wonderful thing happens.

We become both more holy and more happy. When we move toward loving God and our wives with the same grace He loves us with, we get to experience a deeper and more fulfilling joy than surface-level, temporary happiness. God designed us to live a life characterized by sacrificial love and service. **God is working every day in our marriages to help us become the men He made us to be.**

A healthy marriage requires that we die to our selfishness on a daily basis. This makes marriage challenging but also an amazing place to learn to love and sacrifice. Marriage is not about finding the perfect person and effortlessly living happily ever after. That's where a lot of guys miss it. Author and theologian Stanley Hauerwas puts it like this:

> *Destructive to marriage is the self-fulfillment ethic that assumes marriage and the family are primarily institutions of personal fulfillment, necessary for us to become "whole" and happy. The assumption is that there is someone just right for us to marry and that if we look closely enough we will find the right person. This moral assumption overlooks a crucial aspect to marriage. It fails to appreciate the fact that we always marry the wrong person.*
>
> *We never know whom we marry; we just think we do. Or even if we first marry the right person, just give it a while and he or she will change. ... The primary challenge of marriage is learning how to love and care for the stranger to whom you find yourself married.*[1]

The beautiful thing about marriage is that it continually invites us to focus on another person and not just ourselves. Two people dying to themselves to serve and love one another. Showing each other the same grace God shows us.

In laying down His life, Christ modeled the kind of sacrificial love we are called to have for our spouses (see Eph. 5:25). Because self-sacrifice is not in our nature, this kind of love can come only from depending on Christ. We can't fake this kind of love. We can't will it to suddenly appear within us. It's there only because of what Christ is doing in us. It's there because of the amazing power of God's grace in our lives. Author Paul Tripp calls God's grace "the most powerful, protective, and beneficial force in the universe."[2] God shares it with us to save us and also so we can share it with others, including, and especially, our wife. **It's not always easy because we are imperfect individuals battling with our own flesh, but Scripture promises that God is always there for us and that if we will draw near to Him, He will draw near to us** (see Jas. 4:8). As He comes near to our own hearts and near to our marriage in His grace, we're empowered to love our wives.

1. Stanley Hauerwas, "Sex and Politics: Bertrand Russell and 'Human Sexuality,'" *Christian Century*, April 19, 1978, 417-22.

2. Paul David Tripp, *A Shelter in the Time of Storm* (Wheaton, IL: Crossway, 2009), 21.

by Brad Duncan

PAINFUL,
PERMANENT MEMORIES.

I STILL REMEMBER EVERY DETAIL OF THAT DAY—WHERE I WAS WHEN I FIRST EXPERIENCED THE PAIN OF THE NEEDLE LACED WITH INK that penetrated my flesh for the first time. I can still hear the music that was playing in the background, can still see the artwork that covered the walls, and can still smell the incense in the room. I can even remember what I was thinking the moment I felt the pain of that first tattoo. Painful. Permanent. Memories.

LOOKING BACK, I RECOGNIZE IT WAS A PIVOTAL SEASON IN MY LIFE. I was in my early 30s; I had been married seven years; and although I didn't know it at the time, my twisted view of marriage was slowly eroding my relationship with my wife. Marriage was all about me. I was a young man full of dreams. Unfortunately, the dreams were less about us and more about me. Looking back, I realize that in my selfishness, my view of my wife was more about using her as leverage to fulfill my dreams and desires in life. She had become a resource to be tapped to help make me feel a sense of accomplishment and fulfillment. I was using her, and she was feeling used.

My goals had led us to Nashville, Tennessee, and I was finally living my dream. I quickly landed a gig playing guitar and toured the world several times over. Due to my touring schedule, I would be gone several weeks at a time, only to be home for a couple of days prior to leaving again. And what happened in that short window I had at home? Dysfunction. For weeks on the road, I had fans—people who really didn't know me—telling me I was awesome and amazing. Here's the problem: a person can only hear that so long before he begins thinking, You know what? I am pretty awesome! So, I would return home with a sense of ego and entitlement to a person who really knew me. Silence. There was no echo of "you are amazing" in my home.

> The problem is, a person can only hear that so long before they begin thinking... "you know what, I am pretty awesome!"

I remember one spring day when my wife shared in tears that she just wanted to share with me about her day. She went so far as to say that I didn't even have to respond to her or give her feedback. She just wanted to share about her life. But I wasn't interested. I was a fool. My marriage was hanging on by a thread, and I didn't even know it.

DEATH
IS EXPERIENCE.

SOME MEN AT OUR CHURCH INVITED ME TO ATTEND A MEN'S GROUP THAT MET ON WEDNESDAY MORNINGS. I wasn't excited to go because it started at 6:00 a.m. and I was convinced that even Jesus wasn't awake at 6:00 am. But when my wife kicked me out of bed at 5:30, I went.

I was still drinking coffee and cleaning the crust out of my eyes when I realized the guy on the stage had been reading my mail. He was addressing the questions I had been asking: "Do I get it?" "Can I see it?" "Do I know what to do?" and "Will I even get it done?" Deep inside I knew the honest answer to every one of those questions was no. And then it happened. I was given a vision for life that was bigger than myself and bigger than anything I had seen before. The strangest thing was its simplicity. Three words: die to live.

> Deep inside I knew that the honest answer to everyone of the questions was...no.

Live

LEARNING TO DIE.

TODAY I AM STILL LEARNING HOW TO DIE. JUST AS JESUS' DEATH ON THE CROSS WASN'T IMMEDIATE, SO MY DEATH HASN'T BEEN OVERNIGHT. BUT BE ASSURED OF THIS: I AM DYING! In my newfound death I am also experiencing more life than I ever imagined. Die to live. It sums up the life of faith and gives me guidance on how to invest in my marriage (which is no longer on cruise control), my children, extended family, friends, and even complete strangers.

In the growing death of my selfish dreams, I have taken on new dreams in life. Now my desire is to love my wife the way Jesus laid down His life for His bride (see Eph. 5:25). Jesus died for His bride! Jesus served His bride. Jesus was present—physically, emotionally, and spiritually—for His bride. Jesus calls out the best in His bride. These are just a few of the things Jesus did for His bride that I am attempting to do daily for my amazing wife. Dying to myself. Serving. Being present. Affirming. These are four things that have transformed my relationship with my wife.

> Dying to myself. Serving. Being present. Affirming. Four things that have transformed my relationship with my wife.

THE ORIGIN OF "DIE TO LIVE" GOES BACK TO THE TEACHINGS OF JESUS. Jesus is smart. Smarter than I am, so I pay attention to what Jesus had to say. In Matthew 16:24 Jesus taught that to be connected to Him relationally would require two things: "If anyone would come after me, let him deny himself and take up his cross and follow me" (ESV). The first is to deny yourself. In other words, quit focusing only on yourself. There is something happening here that's bigger than you! Now that is difficult enough, but Jesus didn't stop there. He went on to say, "Let him … take up his cross and follow me" (ESV). He taught that a death must take place in the way we live our lives. This includes our dreams, our values, our priorities— every aspect of our lives leading up to the death of our identity as we have known it. At that place we are given a new identity in Christ, complete with new dreams, values, and motivations that enable us to live the life we had always hoped for, always aspired to experience, yet could never attain. What a paradox this is! To truly experience life, we must first die.

THAT MORNING WRECKED ME. I had come face-to-face with a young man who was in desperate need.

Today, we are madly in love with each other. When she sees me doing little things, like taking out the trash or doing the dishes, she knows I am attempting to die a little in my service to her. My wife knows when I ask her how her day was, that I really mean it and honestly want to know about her life. My wife knows just how beautiful she is and what a good mother she is because she is constantly reminded of her value by words of affirmation.

Today I am no longer a musician, but here is the interesting thing. On a good day if you walk into my house and listen closely, you can hear the echo of "You are amazing!" The difference today is the context. It is no longer about Brad; it is about Jesus. Jesus is truly amazing. I am a lover of Jesus. I am growing in my identity as a son of Jesus. I am eternally grateful that Jesus has met me in my need, is teaching me daily to die, and, in exchange, is leading me into life itself.

I still remember where I was when I felt the pain of the needle with my first tattoo, but that isn't my favorite tattoo. My favorite tattoo has a deeper story. It is the story of a 30-something boy who became a man and began to live for something bigger than himself. **MY FAVORITE TATTOO HAS THREE SIMPLE WORDS. "DIE TO LIVE."**

MARRIAGE

FOUR FOUNDATIONAL TRUTHS

1. MARRIAGE WAS GOD'S IDEA.

2. GOD SAID THAT IT WAS NOT GOOD FOR MAN TO BE ALONE.

3. GOD CREATED A HELPER SUITABLE FOR MAN.

4. GOD INTENDED FOR A MAN TO LEAVE HIS PARENTS' HOME AND CLEAVE TO HIS WIFE.

GOD'S DESIGN FOR MARRIAGE

WIVES, SUBMIT TO YOUR OWN HUSBANDS ... AS THE CHURCH SUBMITS TO CHRIST.

HUSBANDS, LOVE YOUR WIVES, AS CHRIST LOVED THE CHURCH AND GAVE HIMSELF UP FOR HER.

EPHESIANS 5:22-25 (ESV)

BASICS

DIE TO LIVE
The Paradox Principle

$\Rightarrow$

DIFFERENT AREAS OF SERVANT LEADERSHIP:

- SPIRITUAL LEADER
- EMOTIONAL ENCOURAGER
- FINANCIAL PROVIDER
- PHYSICAL PROTECTOR

BIBLICAL ROLES

↓↓↓

HUSBAND'S ROLE:
SERVANT LEADER
TO SERVE HIS WIFE IN LOVE AND HUMILITY

WIFE'S ROLE:
DIVINE SUBMISSION
TO LOVE AND RESPECT HER HUSBAND BY AFFIRMING HIS LEADERSHIP

SCRIPTURE REFERENCES

Matthew 22:37-39 (ESV) "Love the Lord your God with all your heart and with all your soul and with all your mind. This is the great and first commandment. And a second is like it: You shall love your neighbor as yourself."

Mark 10:43-45 (ESV) "... Whoever would be great among you must be your servant. ... For even the Son of Man came not to be served but to serve, and to give his life as a ransom for many."

Luke 9:23-24 (ESV) "If anyone would come after me, let him deny himself and take up his cross daily and follow me. For whoever would save his life will lose it, but whoever loses his life for my sake will save it."

Ephesians 5:25 (ESV) "Husbands, love your wives, as Christ loved the church and gave himself up for her."

Philippians 2:3 (ESV) "Do nothing from selfish ambition or conceit, but in humility count others more significant than yourselves."

Philippians 2:4-7 (ESV) "Let each of you look not only to his own interests, but also to the interests of others. Have this mind among yourselves, which is yours in Christ Jesus, who, though he was in the form of God, did not count equality with God a thing to be grasped, but emptied himself, by taking the form of a servant."

Colossians 3:13 (ESV) "... As the Lord has forgiven you, so you also must forgive."

1 Timothy 5:8 (ESV) "If anyone does not provide for his relatives, and especially for members of his household, he has denied the faith and is worse than an unbeliever."

1 Peter 3:7 (ESV) "... Live with your wives in an understanding way."

SUPPORTING RESOURCES

Baucham, Voddie, Jr. *What He Must Be: If He Wants to Marry My Daughter*. Wheaton, IL: Crossway, 2009. In this book on manhood, pastor Voddie Baucham lays out what it means to be a godly man who is ready for marriage.

Hood, Jason B. *Imitating God in Christ: Recapturing a Biblical Pattern*. Downers Grove, IL: InterVarsity Press, 2013. Scholar Jason Hood offers a convincing case that the imitation of Jesus is a key command of the New Testament and a trustworthy guide for how Christians should engage life.

Ramsey, Dave. *The Total Money Makeover: A Proven Plan for Financial Fitness*. Nashville: Thomas Nelson, 2013. Financial guru Dave Ramsey lays out the seven baby steps to financial health. This is a great place to start if you're looking for guidance on how to be the financial leader in your home.

The content in the previous resources does not necessarily reflect that opinion of Authentic Manhood. Readers should utilize these resources but form their own opinions.

Friendship

SESSION **THREE** | Training Guide

| Training Guide OUTLINE

Friendship Presented by John Bryson

I. INTRODUCTION

1. "Happy marriages are based on a deep _____. ... These couples tend to know each other intimately."—Dr. John Gottman[1]

2. God tells us in Genesis 2:18 (ESV) that "... it is not good that the man should be alone ..."

3. Song of Solomon 5:16 (ESV) "... this is my beloved and this is my friend."

4. Part of our role in marriage is to reject relational _____, take the initiative, and cultivate a great friendship with our wife.

II. KEY CHARACTERISTICS OF GREAT FRIENDSHIP IN MARRIAGE

1. Time _____

   • You are _____ looking for opportunities to create some time together, just the two of you.

   • Create unique _____ experiences.

2. Mutual _____

   • Become a lifelong _____ of your wife.

   • Give your wife the gift of having a husband who is endlessly fascinated and intrigued by her and who never ceases to know her better in every way.

   • Looking back is fertile ground for a _____ friendship in marriage.

1. John M. Gottman, *The Seven Principles for Making Marriage Work* (New York: Harmony Books, 2000), 19–20.

3. Mutual _____

- Trust is built on faithfulness to each other.

- Trust also includes confidentiality about things _____ within the marriage.

- Trust includes having each other's _____ in mind.

4. Grace

- In marriage, grace acknowledges the _____ that you are a broken man married to a broken woman.

- A grace-giving husband doesn't try to _____ his wife but loves her as she grows and matures.

- Grace says, "Let's start over" ... maybe even multiple times.

5. Oneness

- Genesis 2:24 (ESV) "... and they shall become one flesh."

- This is a oneness that is spiritually, emotionally, financially, and relationally moving from two individual agendas to one _____ agenda.

- There is plenty of room in the friendship of marriage for individuality.

SESSION THREE | FRIENDSHIP

III. THREE DIFFERENT WAYS OF RELATING WITH OUR WIVES

1. Back-to-back

    • You're in _____ places doing different things with different people.

    • Even as you go your _____ ways, you have a partner out there who's supporting you, thinking of you, and praying for you even when you're not around.

2. Shoulder-to-shoulder

    • So much of marriage will involve you just getting things done _____ your wife.

    • Some shoulder-to-shoulder activity can even include the two of you being together but not necessarily having a lot of face-to-face _____.

3. Face-to-face

    • This is when you are _____ engaged with her. You are focused on listening to her and sharing with her.

    • Creating face-to-face time with the lady you chose to marry is one of the greatest privileges we have as a servant leader.

    • Your wife needs be able to share her heart with you, but she also needs to hear _____ heart.

Be sure to check out Paul Tripp's great marriage resources at paultripp.com and on Twitter @PaulTripp.

PAGE 46

DISCUSSION / REFLECTION QUESTIONS

1. Talk about the difference between loving your spouse and liking your spouse.

2. John mentioned five characteristics of friendship in marriage—time together, mutual curiosity, mutual trust, grace, and oneness. How is your marriage doing in each of these areas?

3. Is there a good balance in your marriage among the different ways you relate with your wife—back-to-back, shoulder-to-shoulder, and face-to-face?

4. Are you an introvert or an extrovert? What about your wife? How does that affect your marriage and the different ways you and your wife relate to each other?

RESOURCES ON THE FOLLOWING PAGES

by Tierce Green

my beloved
&
MY FRIEND

It's only one sentence and a short one at that. But it would be foolish to skip over this vital wisdom about a healthy marriage relationship that is embedded in the colorful and even steamy narrative of the Song of Solomon. In chapter 5, verse 16, the wife describes her husband as her beloved and her friend.

I was in my twenties when I discovered three Greek words for **love**:

Eros is the physical, sensual love. (This word is not actually found in the Bible; however, it is vividly described in The Song of Songs.)

Phileo is the kind of love between friends, or brotherly love.

Then there is *agape*, the selfless, sacrificial, unconditional kind of love. Agape perfectly describes the love God has for us.

As this was presented to me, it seemed that agape was the only kind of love worthy of pursuit.

THAT'S A BIG MISTAKE, ESPECIALLY IN A MARRIAGE.

You might begin to think that you are commanded to love your wife, but you don't have to like her!

Dr. John Gottman, one of the foremost marriage experts in the world, concurs with the wisdom of the wife in the Song of Solomon. After studying over six hundred married couples, he concluded:

"Happy marriages are based on a deep friendship.

By this I mean a mutual respect for and enjoyment of each other's company. These couples tend to know each other intimately—they are well versed in each other's likes, dislikes, personality quirks, hopes, and dreams. They have an abiding regard for each other and express this fondness not just in the big ways but in little ways day in and day out."[1]

A holistic understanding of the Scriptures and how all the truth of God's Word applies to marriage is critical. For instance, the phrase "This is my beloved, this is my friend" (Song 5:16 NIV) from the Song of Solomon reminds me of the words of Jesus when He said, "Greater love has no one than this: to lay down one's life for one's friends" (John 15:13 NIV). From there I see a connection to this: "Love must be sincere. … Be devoted to one another in love. Honor one another above yourselves" (Rom. 12:9-10 NIV). There are hundreds of Scriptures like these that don't specifically mention the topic of marriage, but they are absolutely relevant.

HOW CAN YOU AMP UP FRIENDSHIP IN YOUR MARRIAGE?

Start by applying all the truth you discover in God's Word, not just specific verses that contain the words marriage, husbands, or wives. ⟶

THE SONG OF SOLOMON

Here are just a few examples:

Philippians 2:3-4 says, "Do nothing out of selfish ambition or vain conceit. Rather, in humility value others above yourselves, not looking to your own interests but each of you to the interests of the others" (NIV). Clearly, there is a sacrificial, agape kind of love in that, but I also see a companionship—the kind of love between friends that motivates you to continually discover each other's interests and enjoy them together. The Bible instructs husbands to love their wives as "Christ loved the church and gave himself up for her" (Eph. 5:25, NIV). That is a noble pursuit, but a husband's primary assignment is not just to physically stand between his wife and harm's way. Sometimes, I think it feels easier to physically die for your wife than it is to go on living and to die to yourself daily, intentionally discovering her needs and interests and putting them above your own.

Colossians 3:13 says, "Bear with each other and forgive one another if any of you has a grievance against someone. Forgive as the Lord forgave you" (NIV). That's what true friends do. Just as God has extended grace to us, now we are extensions of His grace to others. Nowhere should that be more evident than between husbands and wives.

In **John 13:14** says, "Now that I, your Lord and Teacher, have washed your feet, you also should wash one another's feet" (NIV). Why wouldn't a husband who loves his wife as Christ loved the church think of applying this principle to his wife first—his beloved and his friend?

Friendship in marriage must be intentionally cultivated. Friends don't automatically grow together, but without attention they can easily grow apart. A loving friendship in marriage can survive many things, but it cannot survive neglect.

My wife and I are closing in on 27 years of marriage. Is that a great marriage? I think it's a really good one. We still have much to learn about being friends. When we were dating, I would sometimes say, "I need to talk to Dana, my friend." Those were times when I needed some unfiltered conversational companionship. As it turned out, that was a big need in her life too. Still is. I love her deeply. She is my beloved and my friend.

---

1. *John M. Gottman,* The Seven Principles for Making Marriage Work *(New York: Harmony, 2000), 19–20. Gottman also discovered that one of the biggest determining factors in whether a couple feels satisfied with the sex, romance, and passion in their marriage is the quality of their friendship.*

1) Back-to-Back

- You're not physically together; you're in different places doing different things.

- You're living the same values and fighting for the same causes.

- You're both seeking the best for your family

- Even as you go, you know you have a partner who's supporting you, thinking of you, and praying for you.

2) Shoulde

- You're both tackling tasks or just doing something together.

- You're getting things done alongside your wife.

3 Different Ways
Relate with You

Understanding and being aware of these three different ways is both perspective-changing and encouraging as we are freed to connect with her in different ways.

...to-Shoulder

- Strategically look for these opportunities to bless your wife.

- You can do things together without necessarily talking a lot.

...to Wife

3) Face-to-Face

- You're directly engaged with, focused on, listening to, and sharing with your wife.

- Some guys can find it challenging and maybe uncomfortable to engage their wives at a heart level.

- Creating this dynamic is one of the greatest privileges you have as a servant leader.

- Embrace the opportunity to hear her heart and share your heart with her.

25 IDEAS to DATE YOUR WIFE

the RED ZONE

ADAPTED FROM: JUSTIN BUZZARD'S DATE YOUR WIFE

with permission from the publisher

1. Serve your wife breakfast in bed.
2. Call your wife in the middle of the day just to say, "I love you."
3. Suprise your wife and clean the house while she is running errands.
4. Make sure you and your wife are in community and on mission with a healthy, gospel-teaching church.
5. Take her out dancing.
6. Lose a marriage fight. Let your wife win.
7. Do something with your wife that both of you are scared to do.
8. Ask your wife about her day and tell her about yours. Do this EVERY DAY.
9. Take dancing lessons with your wife.
10. Detect the one thing you do that most annoys your wife and stop it.
11. Cancel work for the day and do something special with your wife.
12. Criticize your wife less. Compliment her more.
13. Make your wife laugh. Say and do things that make her laugh.
14. Shower with your wife.
15. Make dinner for your wife.
16. Set a weekly date night. Rotate going out and staying in.
17. Tell your wife you love her. OFTEN.
18. Tell your wife that Jesus loves her more than you do.
19. After your next fight, don't make up; make out. See if making out takes care of the making up.
20. Hold your wife's hand often, in public and in private.
21. Create a photo album with some of your most cherished moments.
22. Brag about your wife in front of other people.
23. Cuddle your wife.
24. Remember things that are important to your wife.
25. Notice when your wife is drained or stressed and step in to help.

SCRIPTURE REFERENCES

Genesis 2:18 (NKJV) "It is not good that man should be alone."

Genesis 2:24 (ESV) "Therefore a man shall leave his father and his mother and hold fast to his wife, and they shall become one flesh."

Song of Solomon 5:16 (ESV) "This is my beloved and this is my friend."

SUPPORTING RESOURCES

Buzzard, Justin. *Date Your Wife.* **Wheaton, IL: Crossway, 2012.** In this highly readable and short book, Buzzard provides husbands with very practical ideas for how to love, serve, and date their wives.

Dodd, Chip. *The Voice of the Heart: A Call to Full Living.* **Nashville: Sage Hill Resources, 2001.** Dr. Chip Dodd provides a guide for understanding and navigating our emotions and experiences. This is a great resource for a man who is trying to improve his face-to-face communication with his wife.

Gottman, John M., and Nan Silver. *The Seven Principles for Making Marriage Work.* **New York: Harmony, 2000.** Though not written from a Christian perspective, *The Seven Principles for Making Marriage Work* provides many helpful insights—including insights on friendship in marriage—from one of the foremost marriage experts in the world.

The content in the previous resources does not necessarily reflect the opinion of Authentic Manhood. Readers should utilize these resources but form their own opinions.

Intimacy

SESSION **FOUR** | Training Guide

Intimacy   Presented by Tierce Green

I. INTRODUCTION

1. We often miss God's intentions for sex in one of two ways:

    • We _____ sex, not giving it enough attention in our marriage.

    • We _____ sex, making it the end-all-be-all of a relationship.

2. This session will answer two big questions:

    1. What's the _____ perspective of sex in marriage?

    2. How does an authentic man have a healthy, vibrant, and fulfilling sex life with his wife?

II. A BIBLICAL PERSPECTIVE OF SEX

1. Sex was God's idea.

    • Genesis 2:24–25 (ESV) "A man shall leave his father and his mother and hold fast to his wife, and they shall become one flesh. And the man and his wife were both naked and were not ashamed."

2. Physical intimacy that God designed for marriage is _____.

    • In Genesis, when God finished creation, he declared "everything good." Genesis 1:31 (ESV)

    • 1 Timothy 4:4 (ESV) "Everything created by God is good, and nothing is to be rejected if it is received with thanksgiving."

3. Scripture tells us that God wants husbands and wives to _____ this gift of sexual intimacy.

   - Proverbs 5:18-19 (ESV) "Let your fountain be blessed, and rejoice in the wife of your youth, a lovely deer, a graceful doe. Let her breasts fill you at all times with delight; be intoxicated always in her love."

   - Song of Solomon 4:5-6 (ESV) "Your two breasts are like two fawns, twins of a gazelle, that graze among the lilies. ... I will go away to the mountain of myrrh and the hill of frankincense."

   - You miss it all if you focus just on the _____ parts.

4. Sex is not only physical but also emotional and spiritual.

   - The Bible never promotes sex as merely a _____ act, but always as reflecting a deeper reality.

   - "Sex engages and expresses the whole personality in such a way as to constitute a unique mode of self-disclosure and self-commitment."[1]—D. S. Bailey

   - When the physical, emotional, and spiritual collide, sex becomes much bigger than just a physical act. It becomes an act of _____.

1. D. S. Bailey, *The Man-Woman Relation in Christian Thought* (London: Longmans, 1959), 9–10, as quoted by Timothy Keller, *The Meaning of Marriage* (New York: Riverhead Books, 2011), 258.

III. HOW DOES AN AUTHENTIC MAN HAVE A HEALTHY AND VIBRANT AND FULFILLING SEX LIFE WITH HIS WIFE?

1. Husband 101: What you need to know about yourself.

    - Many men experience a _____ of their lives when their sex drive is powerful and persistent.

    - This powerful and persistent sex drive is normal.

    - Your sex drive is something you want to learn to _____.

    - It's absolutely essential that you and your wife are talking openly and honestly about what each of you feel and desire.

    - As a man, your tendency is going to be to focus on the visual and the _____.

      ° "Men are primarily aroused by visual stimulation. They are excited by feminine nudity or partial nudity. Women, on the other hand, are typically much less visually oriented than men."[2]—Dr. James Dobson

      ° God _____ you to delight in your wife's body.

    - Real sexual fulfillment for men is impossible unless they can sexually fulfill their wives.

2. James Dobson, "More Differences Between Male and Female Sex Drives," Dr. James Dobson's Family Talk [online, cited 22 September 2014]. Available from the Internet: *http://drjamesdobson.org/Solid-Answers/Answers?a=f4a69701-f4da-4f73-bb5f-d5514817814f#sthash.O4qL8qAE.dpuf.*

2. Wife 101: How can you be a servant leader to your wife in your sex life?

   i. Make it your primary goal in sex to _____ rather than to be served.

      • "Die to Live" applies to a man's sex life!

         • The ideal sex life in the Bible is not seeking to get your own needs met, but rather a married man and woman seeking to serve one another.

         • The husband should fulfill his wife's sexual needs, and the wife should fulfill her husband's needs. 1 Corinthians 7:3 (NLT)

   ii. _____ her with words and displays of affection.

   iii. Know what brings _____, both emotional and physical, for your wife.

   iv. Establish a track record of being safe in bed.

      • If she is not_____, then we are not doing that.

   v. Don't rush or overly concentrate on the hot spots.

   vi. Keep growing in your sexual _____ and insight.

   vii. Seek outside help for sexual _____ you can't work through.

   viii. Pray about your sex life together.

Be sure to check out Paul Tripp's great marriage resources at paultripp.com and on Twitter @PaulTripp.

A MAN AND HIS MARRIAGE | PAGE 63

DISCUSSION / REFLECTION QUESTIONS

1. Would you describe your sex life as healthy, vibrant, and fulfilling? Why or why not?

2. Whether married or single, what did you find most insightful or helpful from this session?

3. Do you cultivate the spiritual and emotional side of your sex life? What can you do to grow in that area?

4. Do you and your wife have conversations about your sex life? Are you open and honest with each other? Why or why not?

RESOURCES ON THE FOLLOWING PAGES

- The Search for the Secret Switch (p. 66–69)

- The Myth of Sexual Incompatibility (p. 70–73)

- THE RED ZONE: Let's Talk Sex (p. 74–75)

the Search for the SECRET SWITCH

BY *Sheila Wray Gregoire*

While mulling over possible topics for this article, I turned to my husband and asked, "Keith, what's the one thing about women that men most want to understand?" He chuckled and replied, "That's easy: how to get their wives in the mood." Then he paused and added, "And let me read it when you're finished."

Ah, yes, what is that elusive switch you can flick to turn women on?

Ah, yes, what is that elusive switch you can flick to turn women on? I wonder whether you men suspect we women have one, whether we're all in a giant conspiracy to hide it from you, sort of like Samson and Delilah in reverse. You ask what our secret is, and we tell you something innocuous, like "Sex begins in the kitchen." So you barbecue steaks and scrub plates, and then you flash us that knowing smile. We sigh and head to bed with a novel.

You ask again, and we tell you something else, like "I need romance." So you bring home flowers and chocolates and put on a jazz CD. We head to bed with the box of chocolates.

Nevertheless, you intrepid explorers don't give up, because you're sure the answer is somewhere! We just resist telling you what it is, because once you know, then like Samson, our power is gone.

Right now you likely feel that your wife has all the power in the relationship. If you have the higher sex drive, then that puts her in the driver's seat. You're forced to jump through hoops just in the hope that she might actually say yes. You guys must think we revel in that power! **We don't. Honest. And if I could share any secret with you, it would be this:**

MORE

We don't actually know what that switch is, either.

We don't actually know what that switch is either. After almost two decades of marriage, I've decided women's sex drives are such a mishmash of competing elements that only God knows what's really going on. We're largely hormonal. We're also emotional. And we're spiritual. Get the right mix, and things fly! If one's out of whack, you're likely out of luck.

But I don't want to leave you even more depressed than you already were, so let me give you a few thoughts that will at least send you in the right direction.

1 Tell Your Wife She's Beautiful

Counting your wife's calories is not cool. Telling her, "I have to be honest, I just don't find you sexy anymore since you had kids" is not cool. Questioning what she orders at a restaurant is not cool.

Insulting her weight is a surefire recipe for disaster in your sex life—and in your marriage. If you want to love her sacrificially and empower her to change, then caress her. Love her. Show her what body parts you adore, because chances are she's way harder on herself than you ever could be.

And if you really would prefer that she lose weight, then do it with her! Suggest you take a walk together after dinner. Start cooking healthful meals. If you don't find her attractive, then you're part of the problem. Be part of the solution too.

2 Touch Her—Without Expecting It to Go Anywhere

Many women stop kissing as soon as they walk down the aisle because too many husbands give their wives the message that kissing equals a promissory note for sex later. If you give that impression, then you've also guaranteed you'll have a lousy sex life.

Why? Because women aren't always sure they want the touch to go somewhere. So they'll stop touching to avoid a fight. But if they stop touching, they eliminate one of the primary ways they feel safe, close, and even desired. You need touch in your relationship if you're going to boost her libido. Start touching and kissing—not groping—your wife regularly.

3 Don't Increase Her Exhaustion

When I wrote *The Good Girl's Guide to Great Sex*, I found that women's number one reason for not wanting sex is that they are absolutely exhausted. We have to be able to concentrate to enjoy making love. If we're tired, we can't concentrate.

If you want more sex, then g out of your way to make sure your wife isn't exhausted.

If you want more sex, then go out of your way to make sure your wife isn't exhausted. Pick up a mop. Put the kids in bed. Help her figure out what commitments she can eliminate. Sometimes she'll resist because most women are control freaks; they get testy if a man tries to help. But push through because she needs to feel she doesn't have the world on her shoulders.

4 Talk to Her

Want more action in the bedroom? Better make sure there's action outside the bedroom too! Just take a walk with her every night and catch up, giving her a chance to share her heart. Ask about her day and what she's worried about. This helps clear her head too so that she won't be so distracted when making love.

5 Figure Out What Feels Good to Her

If your wife isn't having a good time in bed, she certainly may have sexual issues. But for the vast majority of women, when sex doesn't feel pleasurable, it's because her husband hasn't taken the time to learn how to make her feel good, and she's given up.

Take time to discover how she likes to be touched (hint: chances are it's a lot lighter than you like to be touched). Many women are embarrassed to tell their husbands what they want, and others may not even know what feels good. Don't take her silence to mean you're doing everything right. If she's not in ecstasy, you have work to do.

6 Trash the Porn

Pornography rewires your brain so that what becomes arousing is a picture or an image rather than a live human being. It will make your wife feel like trash, and it will make her feel angry and unwanted. It is not OK. It is not harmless. It is not something you do just to give your wife a break sometimes. It is wrong. Always. End of story.

7 Clean Is Sexy

Often the best foreplay is a shower. If you're stinky, she won't want to get near you. If you're a guy who has never really enjoyed brushing his teeth and considers showering a waste of time, then it's time to re-evaluate your priorities.

> It isn't only about doing what you want; it's also being kind to those around you.

It isn't only about doing what you want; it's also being kind to those around you. And if you're turning her off, it will be a lot harder to turn her on.

8 Love Her Anyway

Will taking these seven steps totally assure your bedroom heats up? Not necessarily. There are no guarantees, and all too many women are insensitive to their husbands' very real sexual needs. But love her anyway. When you aren't getting your needs met, the answer isn't to withdraw. Love, acceptance, and selflessness can turn a marriage around. And even if they don't, you've stepped out in faith to love her as Jesus called you to (see Eph. 5:25). If your wife doesn't notice or appreciate it, rest assured that God always does.

Sheila Wray Gregoire delivers "Girl Talk" events across the country to help women learn more about what God intends for sex in marriage. She's the author of The Good Girl's Guide to Great Sex, *and she blogs everyday at* http://tolovehonorandvacuum.com.

The Myth of Sexual Incompa

by Shelia Wray Gregoire

Can Christians Be Sexually Incompatible?

Increasingly, I've seen this argument in articles and in discussions with people: because Christians aren't supposed to have sex before we're married, there's no way to know whether two people are sexually compatible. And lots of people just aren't compatible, so sex won't work well for them.

The answer then suggested is either divorce, giving up on sex altogether, or abandoning God's design for faithfulness and monogamy.

But what if the whole idea of sexual incompatibility is a rabbit trail to begin with?

When we claim that two people are sexually incompatible, we're saying he's one way, and she's another, and together they don't match. That approach assumes we are sexual beings in and of ourselves, separate from another person. Each person has a static sexuality, so when two come together, they don't fit.

> What if sex was never intended to be "She's like that, and he's like that" but rather "Together we're like this"?

tibility

What if sex was never intended to be "She's like that, and he's like that" but rather "Together we're like this"?

I think the together model is far closer to the truth. Yes, we are each born with certain sexual drives. In fact, our sexuality and our spirituality are very closely linked, because with both sexuality and spirituality we have a deep need and a deep drive to be intimate and known.

And it's that *known* word that's really important. Sex is supposed to be a deep knowing between two people. It isn't that two people come together and use each other to get their sexual needs met; it's that our sexuality is supposed to be expressed with another person. Our sexuality is, at heart, relational.

Our sexuality is, at heart, relational.

People used to understand this, but if you think about it, it makes sense only if you also believe sex belongs inside a marriage. As soon as you take sex outside a committed marriage relationship, as our culture has done, then the only permanent thing in your sex life is you. To make sex great, then, you just need to learn what you want, not how you both work together. **If we start saying two people can be sexually incompatible, then we're buying into our culture's view that sex is something that is supposed to be experienced with many people.** Since partners are constantly changing, you are the only constant. Thus, knowing ourselves sexually isn't about the married couple; it's only about you. This is not the way God designed sex to be.

Being "Sexually Incompatible" Is Simply a Marriage Issue That Needs to Be Dealt With

In truth, sexual incompatibility simply means something is not working well in your marriage. And honestly, that's quite normal. **We all have baggage when we get married, and because our sexuality is so close to our spirituality, it's deeply personal and more difficult to deal with than a lot of other conflicts.** But that doesn't mean we can't deal with it!

It took my husband and me six years to figure out this part of our marriage because I had difficulty trusting, and frankly, sex didn't feel wonderful. It would have been easy for us to say we were sexually incompatible—that his libido was higher than mine and that I was too frigid for him. But instead, we treated it like a problem that had to be dealt with. Gradually, we grew together, and things got better.

That's how it is in most marriages. When I wrote *The Good Girl's Guide to Great Sex*, I surveyed thousands of women and found that the best years for sex in a marriage are years 16 through 24. They aren't the early years. It takes a while to get things right. But if we believe in sexual incompatibility, then it's all too easy to say, "There's no point in trying. We weren't meant to go together."

What If Sexual Differences Push Us Toward More Holiness?

Often when we say we're not sexually compatible, it's because one person wants sex more than the other. We tend to think it's the guy, but in about one-quarter of marriages, the woman has the higher libido, and she's left wondering why her husband doesn't want her.

Yet what if libido differences are actually a vehicle God uses to push us toward more holiness? One of us more naturally bends toward self-control, and one of us more naturally bends toward passion. Both are good things. And these libido differences help stretch us, so that the one with more self-control learns more passion, and the one with more passion learns more self-control.

Sometimes sexual incompatibility is less about libido and more about one person being more adventurous than the other. Again, this isn't an incompatibility issue. It's simply a tool that can help push us toward holiness. We may need to communicate and ask for what we want; we may need to step outside our comfort zone and find real passion; we may need to confront deep-seated fantasies and recognize that these are from harmful sources. Whatever the issue, your spouse isn't the problem. It's simply something to work through together by becoming

> It's simply something to work through together by becoming more vulnerable, more humble, and more passionate.

more vulnerable, more humble, and more passionate. And those are all good things too!

The only area where there could be true incompatibility—an area where working on something will not make it better—is if health issues are involved. Perhaps one of you is paralyzed, has had cancer, or has chronic pain. Perhaps your wife has vaginismus (pain during intercourse). Some of these conditions can get better, but others are for life.

But, is that incompatibility? Or is this part of the "in sickness and in health" bit of your marriage vows? Yes, it's heartbreaking. And yes, it's not what either of you signed up for. **But sometimes in marriage we don't get what we expect, and in those times God is always big enough to see you through.**

If we look at most sexual problems—whether one person wants sex all the time and one person never wants it or whether one person wants weird things while someone else is too scared to stray from the missionary position—the root tends to be either woundedness or brokenness.

When you're wounded because someone has abused you or shamed you, your sexuality will be affected. When you're broken because you've sinned and your sexuality has been misdirected, then the problem is not your wife; the problem is your heart.

God is in the healing business, and He loves to take those who are wounded and broken and restore them to wholeness. **Perhaps our sexuality is an area where God can most clearly reveal to us that we need Him. Having sexual issues does not mean we can't fit together. It just means we both need more of God to heal us from our past decisions, mistakes, and shame and to give us a clear path forward.**

Being "Sexually Incompatible" Can Be Fixed!

In most cases, then, sexual incompatibility isn't true incompatibility. It's not permanent; it's simply something you need to fix. And fixing it may push you out of your comfort zone. You have to confront your own baggage. You have to communicate about tough issues. You have to compromise and adjust. You need to confess any sin and seek forgiveness. But these are all good things, and they're all a normal part of marriage.

If you believe the compatibility myth that sex should be easy and two people should work together right from the start, you're likely to be disappointed. That's not how we were made.

But we weren't made to have permanent problems either. As we work through what we want in the bedroom, we tend to have stronger marriages in all ways. We compromise, we communicate, and we pray. Strong marriages are built on those actions.

> We compromise, we communicate, we pray. Strong marriages are built on those things.

So don't give up on your marriage just because you feel you aren't sexually compatible. Treat this like any other problem and start to deal with it. You may just find that you both grow together after all!

questions every man should ask his wi

LET'S TALK
SEX

HERE ARE SOME GOOD QUESTIONS TO ASK IN ORDER TO GET A CONVERSATION STARTED WITH YOUR WIFE ABOUT EXPECTATIONS IN THE BEDROOM.

X **What does "normal" look like for us as a couple?**

X **How often are we going to have sex?**

X **What are our expectations of each other regarding physical intimacy?**

X **What are your wants, needs, and desires in the bedroom?**

X **Do I make you feel loved and cared for in the bedroom?**

X **Do we experience God's blessings and grace in our intimacy?**

SCRIPTURE REFERENCES

Genesis 2:24–25 (ESV) "A man shall leave his father and his mother and hold fast to his wife, and they shall become one flesh. And the man and his wife were both naked and were not ashamed."

Genesis 1:31 (ESV) "God saw everything that he had made, and behold, it was very good."

Proverbs 5:18–19 (ESV) "Let your fountain be blessed, and rejoice in the wife of your youth, a lovely deer, a graceful doe. Let her breasts fill you at all times with delight; be intoxicated always in her love."

Song of Solomon 4:5–6 (ESV) "Your two breasts are like two fawns, twins of a gazelle, that graze among the lilies. ... I will go away to the mountain of myrrh and the hill of frankincense."

1 Corinthians 7:3 (NLT) "The husband should fulfill his wife's sexual needs, and the wife should fulfill her husband's needs."

1 Timothy 4:4 (ESV) "Everything created by God is good, and nothing is to be rejected if it is received with thanksgiving."

SUPPORTING RESOURCES

Budziszewski, J. *On the Meaning of Sex*. Wilmington, DE: Intercollegiate Studies Institute, 2012. Budziszewski, a professor of government and philosophy at the University of Texas at Austin, challenges our modern culture's view of sex.

Cutrer, William, and Sandra Glahn. *Sexual Intimacy in Marriage*. 3rd ed. Grand Rapids: Kregel, 2007. Written by a medical doctor and a theologian, *Sexual Intimacy in Marriage* provides a great overview of both the purpose and technique of sex in marriage.

Gregoire, Shelia Wray. *The Good Girl's Guide to Great Sex*. Grand Rapids: Zondervan, 2012. Shelia Wray Gregoire offers insightful advice for how Christian women can enjoy sex in marriage.

The content in the previous resources does not necessarily reflect the opinion of Authentic Manhood. Readers should utilize these resources but form their own opinions.

Threats

SESSION **FIVE** | Training Guide

Training Guide OUTLINE

Threats <small>Presented by John Bryson</small>

I. INTRODUCTION

1. Authentic men need to be _____ of these threats, know how they operate, and take precautions to avoid them.

II. FIVE MARRIAGE THREATS

1. Sex

   • Proverbs 6:27 (ESV) "Can a man carry fire next to his chest and his clothes not be burned?"

   • God _____ the intimacy and the flames of sex to burn safely within a life-long commitment between a husband and a wife.

   • Internet Pornography

      o The Bible tells us to "_____ from sexual immorality."
        1 Corinthians 6:18 (ESV)

      o We learned in Volume 3 that we have to fight fire with fire by fully embracing the power of God's _____ and turning our hearts to His more satisfying promises.

      o One of the greatest gifts you can give your wife or future wife is to be a man who fights for purity.

   • Premarital Sex

      o When sex precedes _____, pain and distrust are the eventual result every time.

      o One of the greatest ways you can show love and build trust is to guard both your and her _____.

- Extramarital Affair[1]

    o Proverbs 6:32 (ESV) "He who commits adultery lacks sense; he who does it destroys himself."

    o An extramarital affair won't even deliver the _____ it promises.

    o They usually start out as an emotional connection but follow a pretty predictable pattern.

        - SEE THE "ANATOMY OF AN AFFAIR" ILLUSTRATION ON PAGES 84–85.

    o The best way to affair-proof your marriage is to keep the fire kindled at home—to cultivate the flames of friendship and intimacy with your wife.

- If you've messed up in any of these areas, there's one word to remember: _____. Jesus died on the cross to offer you grace, forgiveness, and the power to change.

    o An Authentic Man confesses, repents, and _____ God with his repentant heart.

A Graceless Home

- A graceless home is when a home or marriage become performance-based and expectations-filled.

- A graceless home will _____ oneness in your marriage.

- You and your spouse will tend toward one of two extremes when faced with conflict:

Some of the content for the section on extramarital affairs was inspired by a sermon preached by Tommy Nelson, the Senior Pastor of Denton Bible Church in Denton, Texas.

o "Fighter": you tend to be aggressive and don't mind verbalizing your frustrations.

o "Bottler": you tend to _____ conflict and escape.

• Proverbs 19:11 (NLT) " Sensible people control their temper; they earn respect by overlooking wrongs."

3. Money

• _____ about money can be a major source of stress in a marriage.

• Financial baggage usually includes:

o Influence from family of origin.

o Personal financial choices.

• It is crucial for spouses to openly and honestly _____ these money issues so they can be on the same page and avoid the major threat that money can become.

4. Kids

• Psalm 127:3 (NLT) says that "children are a gift from the LORD."

- There are usually two types of misses when it comes to kids:

    o Selfishness: this is when a married couple neglects or pays too little attention to the kids.

    o Too much attention: this is when the marriage becomes kid-centric at the expense of the married couple's relationship.

5. Identity

- This is when a husband tries to find his ultimate _____ , value, or worth in his marriage or his wife.

- No wife can be perfect, and she's not designed or equipped to be our _____.

- Authentic Men love their wives deeply and neither overly-depend on nor act completely independent of their spouse.

Be sure to check out Paul Tripp's great marriage resources at paultripp.com and on Twitter @PaulTripp.

A MAN AND HIS MARRIAGE | PAGE 81

DISCUSSION / REFLECTION QUESTIONS

1. Are you finding that you and your wife are more susceptible to some of these particular threats more than others?

2. How are you doing with sex-related threats (porn, premarital, extramarital)? What are some precautions you have taken or need to take to avoid those threats?

3. Discuss what an authentic friendship with a woman who's not your wife should look like?

4. When it comes to conflict, are you a "fighter" or a "bottler"? What about your wife? How can understanding these tendencies help you and your wife deal with conflict?

5. Is your home defined by grace? Do you create space for your wife to make mistakes?

AUTHENTIC MANHOOD
MANHOOD
YOUR **STRATEGIC MOVE**

RESOURCES ON THE FOLLOWING PAGES

- Anatomy of an Affair (p. 84–85)

- Cheap Shots in Marriage (p. 86–89)

- **THE RED ZONE:** Unity in Finances (p. 90–91)

№ 1
Neglect

Unintentional neglect of each other in your marriage. Both the friendship and the physical intimacy begin to wane.

№ 2
Affirmation

Someone of the opposite sex is really kind to you. She notices you, compliments you, affirms you, and makes you feel respected.

№ 3
Enjoyment

The compliment turns into a conversation. Maybe a lunch together. Your time feels good and is meeting a need.

ANATOMY
OF AN AFFAIR

№ 5
Ongoing Contact

You exchange contact information and begin staying connected, calling and texting each other. You begin covering your tracks. You start convincing yourself that things would be better with her than your wife.

№ 6
False Reality

Seeing her only when she's at her best, you fail to realize your view of her is skewed. Because you're acting alone, you don't have any trusted friends who can help bring you back to reality.

№ 4
Emotional Investment

You find yourself attracted and begin sharing your heart with her. You start laughing and sharing secrets together. You begin justifying the relationship to yourself.

№ 7
Physical Intimacy

The emotional connection becomes physical intimacy.

The heart A, the right ventricle; B, the left ventricle; C, the right auricle; D, the left auricle.

CHEAP SHOTS

★ IN MARRIAGE ★

by Brian Goins

June 28, 1997

It was the most heavily anticipated boxing rematch since the "Thrilla in Manilla" between Ali and Frazier.

Held at the MGM Grand Garden Arena in Las Vegas, Nevada, and billed as "The Sound and the Fury," it pitted "Iron" Mike Tyson against Evander "The Real Deal" Holyfield for the second time in seven months. In the first bout, Holyfield overcame 25-to-1 odds to beat the number-one-ranked heavyweight. Over two million homes ponied up the cash for pay-per-view to watch Mike exact revenge.

Instead, they saw him exact an ounce or two of flesh.

With about a minute left to go in the third round, Iron Mike clamped his teeth on Evander's ear. The announcer said, "I think Tyson just bared his teeth. This is turning into a street fight." The world was shocked.

The outrage wasn't because two men were punching each other in the face. We celebrate, cheer, and enjoy

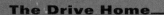

- HEAVYWEIGHT -

a good fight. It's only when one fighter decides to go below the belt or, rather, above the lobe, that the battle prompts our outrage.

CHEAP SHOTS TAKE THE FIGHT OUT OF A GOOD FIGHT. THE SAME THING IS TRUE IN MARRIAGE. Ever since another unfortunate biting incident (Adam and Eve), couples have been stepping into the ring engaging in relational fist cuffs. And nothing takes the fight out of a good marital fight like landing a few cheap shots at our spouse.

The Drive Home

It takes 3 hours and 32 minutes to drive from Atlanta to Charlotte. I know this because for 3 hours and 32 minutes the only thing I said to my wife was "What do you think your kids want for dinner tonight?"

Our weekend had been spent sparring over a decision we both felt very strongly about. In the bout we had thrown a few sarcastic left hooks and snide jabs. When we strapped on the seat belts to head home, rather than use those hours in the car to deal with the issue or seek reconciliation, I pummeled Jen with the cheap shot I made famous—the silent haymaker. I punish with silence until I feel ready to pounce.

What are your go-to cheap shots? Silence? Shouting? Rehashing the past? Comparison? Generalizations (noted by the use of *always* or *never)?* Character defamation ("You've never respected what I do!")? Kitchen-sinking (using a flurry of verbal punches, sighs, and eye rolling to keep the spouse backpedaling)?

ANYTIME YOU PUT TWO SINNERS UNDER ONE ROOF, THERE WILL BE CONFLICT. BUT ONCE YOU RESORT TO CHEAP SHOTS, THE FOCUS MOVES QUICKLY FROM RECONCILIATION TO RETALIATION. James says, "So also the tongue is a small member, yet it boasts of great things. How great a forest is set ablaze by such a small fire!" (Jas. 3:5 ESV).

★ How do you resolve fights when the cheap shots start flying?

Who's in Your Corner?

Sixteen years after "the bite seen round the world," Evander and Mike fielded questions from Larry King. Evander said after Mike tore off a part of his ear, he was "angry, and I was going to bite him back." But despite the cacophony that had erupted, Holyfield heard his corner man, Tim, yell, "Keep your mind on the Lord!"

With those few words, the trainer changed the direction of the fight. He transported Evander from the ring to a hillside where Jesus outlined a fighting strategy for parrying cheap shots: "You have heard that it was said, 'An eye for an eye and a tooth for a tooth [reasonable to insert 'an ear for an ear'].' BUT I SAY TO YOU, DO NOT RESIST THE ONE WHO IS EVIL. BUT IF ANYONE SLAPS YOU ON THE RIGHT CHEEK, TURN TO HIM THE OTHER ALSO" (MATT. 5:38-39 ESV).

- FLYWEIGHT -

It goes against our very fiber. It feels like we're throwing in the towel. Giving up. And yet Jesus is showing us a better way. HE KNOWS CHEAP SHOT FOR CHEAP SHOT HAS A 100% FAIL RATE. Anytime I resort to jabbing Jen with silent haymakers or undercutting her with shouts, I never walk away from those fights thinking, "Now that was a solid strategy. You really showed her that time, Goins." I am ashamed, Jen is hurt, the kids are shocked, and my marriage suffers.

The apostle Paul prepared the church in Romans with relational pugilism tips similar to Jesus' words: "Repay no one evil for evil, but give thought to do what is honorable in the sight of all. If possible, so far as it depends on you, live peaceably with all. Beloved, never avenge yourselves, but leave it to the wrath of God. ... Do not be overcome by evil, but overcome evil with good" (Rom. 12:17-21 ESV).

Peter, who evidently preferred swords over fists, put it simply, "Do not repay evil with evil or insult with insult" (1 Pet. 3:9 NIV). This verse follows right after Peter wrote his wisdom to spouses (1 Pet. 3:1-7). Something tells me Peter, who was married and never had a thought he didn't share, delivered a few below-the-belt invectives.

★ So how do you "keep your mind on the Lord" when the cheap shots start flying in marriage?

Remember, You've Got a Trainer

Listen to your Trainer. Evander heard many voices as the blood trickled down his neck. The crowds gasped and then screamed for him to fight back. He heard Iron Mike taunting, "Come on! Bring it!" His heart shouted, "Go bite that ..." But he listened only to his trainer, Tim.

WHEN WE ARE IN A FIGHT, MULTIPLE VOICES SCREAM FOR OUR ATTENTION, BUT IF YOU ARE A FOLLOWER OF JESUS, YOU ARE CALLED TO LISTEN TO ONE. Jesus said to the disciples that when He left, He would send a "Helper"—a Trainer—for us, the Holy Spirit, who would "teach you all things and bring to your remembrance all that I have said to you" (John 14:26 ESV).

When I was riding in that van from Atlanta to Charlotte, I heard my Trainer for 3½ hours remind me of my role as the lead initiator in the home. He called me to be a peacemaker, not a conflict avoider. He shouted at me, "Brian, that's God's daughter you're treating like trash in front of your kids. Is that how you want them thinking a man treats his wife?" I heard His voice; I just obeyed my own. I wasn't stupid. I was just stubborn.

THE BEAUTY OF THE GOSPEL IS THAT GOD WANTS TO DO IN US WHAT WE CANNOT DO IN OURSELVES. We have a trainer, the Holy Spirit, who not only reminds us of who we are, but empowers us to love our spouse like God loves us. God turned the other cheek. He took the blows. He absorbed the pain so we could gain.

Remember the Ground Rules

Every boxing match has a referee who makes sure the boxers fight a clean fight. Unfortunately, when two spouses start a fight, there's no ref who jumps out of the pantry and stops the fight after a cheap shot, so it's always good for you and your wife to establish some agreed-upon ground rules for how you will deal with conflict.

Here are a few suggestions:

★ Avoid generalizations *(always/never).*

★ Focus on one issue rather than many.

★ Keep in-laws, or others, out of the argument.

★ Keep the past in the past.

★ Seek to understand your spouse before you expect them to understand you.

When it comes to verbal sparring, James shows how to adjust the speed of our punches: "Be quick to listen, slow to speak and slow to become angry" (1:19 NIV). To fight fair, I must be quick, slow, slow. But if you watch my cheap shots, you will notice I'm always slow, quick, quick: slow to listen, quick to speak, and quick to anger. Before you find yourself in another squabble, train your brain to ask three simple questions before you speak: "Will these words I'm about to say help or harm? Am I trying to retaliate or restore? Am I pursuing peace or punishing?"

Remember What's at Stake

In professional boxing, when one person wins, even the loser walks away with millions. Tyson broke the rules and still raked in 30 million for that fight. In marriage, when one spouse wins a fight, both walk away losers, and the marriage pays the tab.

Paul reminds us in Ephesians, "We do not wrestle against flesh and blood" (6:12 ESV). Earlier in the letter he said, "Be angry and do not sin; do not let the sun go down on your anger, and give no opportunity to the devil" (4:26-27 ESV).

This doesn't mean "stay up and fight." PAUL IS CALLING EVERY BELIEVER TO RESOLVE CONFLICT QUICKLY BECAUSE WHEN WE LET IT LINGER OR RESORT TO CHEAP SHOTS, ONLY ONE WINS: THE DEVIL. Satan can't harm God. So he's been marring the "living picture" of God (marriage) since page 3 of Scripture. And his strategy is simple. When he convinces believers to return insult for insult, it's like spraying graffiti all over God's image on earth. People see God clearly when believers take it on the chin in the name of love (see 1 John 4: 7-12). When couples choose to return a blessing for an insult and value the relationship more than revenge, their kids get a snapshot of God.

The Road Back

After we finally arrived at home from Atlanta, our anger seethed as the sun sank. The next day, the kids left for school, and I felt like a boxer walking through the crowds. Practicing my punches. Eyes transfixed. We approached center ring, and Jen said, "Brian, before we begin, I just need to say something. I'm sorry. Would you forgive me? I know I've got strong feelings about this, but there was no excuse for the way I treated you. Let's resolve this and move on."

I wanted to scream, "NO! I'm ready to fight!"

I WANTED TO SCREAM.

The Trainer was immediately in my ear: "Brian, she beat you to the punch. Who should have been first to apologize? Who should have initiated reconciliation rather than nursed revenge?" She took the fall so our relationship would win.

November 21, 2013

Mike Tyson knocked on Evander's door and said, "I'm sorry, Evander." He handed him a little box. "It's your ear."

The Foot Locker commercial ended by saying, "It seems like everything is right with the world." Sixteen years after the "bite seen round the world," one of the most shocking cheap shots in sports was finally resolved.

Fortunately, they weren't married.

HOW LONG WILL YOU WAIT TO RESTORE THE RELATIONSHIP? SOMEONE BACK IN THE CORNER OF YOUR HEART IS SHOUTING, "KEEP YOUR MIND ON THE LORD!"

UNITY IN FINANCE

by Mike Boschetti

I couldn't believe it. What was supposed to be the process of building our dream house was anything but a dream; it was a nightmare. We were constantly having conflict. It should not have been this way. When we found the perfect five-acre lot in the country and before meeting with the builder, I took the equity in the house we had just sold and our budget; figured out the maximum amount we could afford for the house; and shared it with my wife, Starr. I should not have been concerned. I know her, and I know how frugal she is. No matter what the budget was, I knew she wouldn't go over it. Why, then, were we having all this conflict? When she excitedly shared with me ideas like stained-glass windows and other extras

she and the builder's architect were coming up with, I was greatly concerned and expressed my discontent in not-so-subtle ways. Fortunately, we were rescued from that nightmare. We had purchased the lot in a new subdivision, and the sale was contingent on finding sufficient water. After a few wells were drilled, the amount of water discovered was inadequate, so we were released from our obligation.

Fast-forward three years. We found more country acreage and began again to build our dream home. This time we built it with zero conflict. What was the difference? This time Starr and I worked on the budget together, and we agreed to a maximum we couldn't exceed, as well as a slightly lower umber that neither of us was comfortable xceeding. The first time around, I never ommunicated that lower maximum to her, so he was operating with a different figure in ind. This time we were on the same page. Ve were unified. As a result, not only did e enjoy the process, but we also came a little under budget.

It is common knowledge that money is a ajor source of conflict in marriage. Why? nances show up in a relationship in many ays. A recent issue of *Money* magazine ontained some statistics illustrating some f those ways. **Not surprisingly, 70 percent f married couples argue about money. Of ose couples, 55 percent say the prob- m is spending, 37 percent claim it's about fferent ideas on saving, and 21 percent bout deceit. Twenty-two percent say they ent money they didn't want their spouse to ow about, and 11 percent say he or she is xcluded from decisions. Spouses don't real- e the real basis of the conflict is differing xpectations. The previous statistics are just ow they are displayed. All of these statis- cs confirm that.**[1]

In the next column are some very ractical things couples can do to be unified nd minimize financial conflict.

Love and Money by the Numbers," *Money* [online], 1 June 2014 [cited 25 September 2014]. Available rom the Internet: *http://time.com/money/2800576/love-money-by-the-numbers/*.

PRACTICAL TIPS
TO MINIMIZE CONFLICT

- Before you can be unified in the use of money, you must be unified in your relationship with God. Couples who are closer to God are closer to each other and therefore have a better chance of discerning God's will for their money.
- Recognize that God is the Owner of all you have, regardless of who earned it or who wants to spend it. The first step, therefore, is to agree together that you are actually man- aging someone else's money—God's.
- Plans give hope. Ultimately, our hope is in God, but working together on a plan to spend money (a budget) provides a way to unify your expec- tations and thus minimize conflict.
- Regardless of who is the primary breadwinner, it is crucial for both spouses to be involved when mak- ing financial decisions. God put two people together to become one, so when one makes any decision with- out input from the other party, that person is in making a decision with half a brain. God gave you the other half to help. Don't ignore it.

SCRIPTURE REFERENCES

Psalm 127:3 (ESV) "Children are a heritage from the LORD, the fruit of the womb a reward."

Proverbs 6:27 (ESV) "Can a man carry fire next to his chest and his clothes not be burned?"

Proverbs 6:32 (ESV) "He who commits adultery lacks sense; he who does it destroys himself."

Proverbs 11:14 (ESV) "Where there is no guidance, a people falls, but in an abundance of counselors there is safety."

Proverbs 19:11 (NLT) "Sensible people control their temper; they earn respect by overlooking wrongs."

1 Corinthians 6:18 (ESV) "Flee from sexual immorality."

SUPPORTING RESOURCES

Cusick, Michael John. *Surfing for God: Discovering the Divine Desire Beneath Sexual Struggle.* Nashville: Thomas Nelson, 2012. This book is one of the better book-length treatments of how to battle sexual temptation and lust.

Harley, Willard F., Jr. *His Needs, Her Needs: Building an Affair-Proof Marriage.* Rev. ed. Grand Rapids, MI: Revell, 2011. In this best seller Harley discusses how understanding the different needs of men and women can help affair-proof a marriage.

Kimmel, Tim. *Grace-Based Parenting.* Nashville: Thomas Nelson, 2004. Kimmel provides an approach to parenting that begins and ends with grace—accepting God's grace to us and then extending grace to our kids.

Ramsey, Dave. *The Total Money Makeover: A Proven Plan for Financial Fitness.* Thomas Nelson, 2013. Financial guru Dave Ramsey lays out the seven baby steps to financial health.

The content in the previous resources does not necessarily reflect the opinion of Authentic Manhood. Readers should utilize these resources but form their own opinions.

Game-Changers

SESSION **SIX** | Training Guide

Game-Changers Presented by Bryan Carter

I. INTRODUCTION

1. In this session we are going to give you 20 practical ideas that can help you "die to live" in your marriage. We call them _____ _____.

II. TWENTY GAME-CHANGERS

1. A servant leader includes his wife in _____ the future.

2. A servant leader accepts the responsibility of spiritual _____ in his marriage.

3. A servant leader is honest with his family and with himself about his own

    _____.

    - "Flawed leaders are successful because they're not preoccupied with protecting their image. ... A limping leader is the kind of person God uses to accomplish amazing things."[1]—Dan Allender, _Leading with a Limp_

4. A servant leader discusses the household responsibilities with his wife and makes sure that they are_____distributed.

5. A servant leader seeks the _____ of his wife on all major financial decisions.

6. A servant leader_____ _____with commitments he has made to his wife.

---

1. Dan Allender, _Leading with a Limp_ (Colorado Springs: WaterBrook, 2006).

7. A servant leader anticipates the different _____ of his marriage.

8. A servant leader manages potential _____ so that he can connect with his wife and family.

9. A servant leader makes sure that he and his wife have a will in place and have arranged a well-conceived _____ in the event of his death.

10. A servant leader develops a healthy relationship with his wife's _____.

11. A servant leader joins a _____ _____ of men who are dedicated to growing as husbands and fathers.

   • Proverbs 27:17 (ESV) "Iron sharpens iron, and one man sharpens another."

12. A servant leader pays attention to the _____ of the home and anticipates any pressure points.

13. A servant leader celebrates and _____ his wife frequently and publicly.

14. A servant leader encourages his wife to _____ as an individual and provides time and resources for her to pursue her own interests.

15. A servant leader expresses his love for his wife in a variety of ways that speak _____ to her.

16. A servant leader points his wife to _____.

17. A servant leader allows his wife to _____ him.

   • "Men who allow their wives to influence them have happier marriages and are less likely to divorce than men who resist their wives' influence."[2]

   —Marriage expert Dr. John Gottman

   • Proverbs 27:9 (ESV) "The sweetness of a friend comes from his earnest counsel."

18. A servant leader initiates family _____ around important celebrations and holidays.

19. A servant leader has learned how to be both _____ and _____.

   • "The husband is called to lead like Jesus who is the Lion of Judah (Rev. 5:5) and the Lamb of God (Rev. 5:6)—he was lionhearted and lamblike, strong and meek, tough and tender, aggressive and responsive, bold and brokenhearted. He sets the pattern for manhood."[3]—Pastor John Piper

20. A servant leader keeps _____ at the center of his marriage.

2. John M. Gottman, *The Seven Principles for Making Marriage Work* (New York: Harmony, 2000), 100.
3. John Piper, *This Momentary Marriage: A Parable of Permanence* (Wheaton, IL: Crossway, 2009), 73–74.

Be sure to check out Paul Tripp's great marriage resources at paultripp.com and on Twitter @PaulTripp.

DISCUSSION/REFLECTION QUESTIONS

Which Game-Changer challenged you the most? Discuss.

What is one thing you can begin doing today to be a better servant leader to your wife?

Game-Changer #3 says an Authentic Man is honest with his family about his own imperfections. What does that look like in your home?

Who are the other men in your life who are truly challenging and encouraging you to be better husband and father (Game-Changer #11)?

Reread the quotation by John Piper: "The husband is called to lead like Jesus who is Lion of Judah and the Lamb of God—he was both lionhearted and lamblike, strong and meek, tough and tender, aggressive and responsive, bold and brokenhearted. He sets pattern for manhood." What does it look like to be both tough and tender as a husband and as a man? What does it look like in your marriage to follow Jesus' example in being both tough and tender for your wife?

AUTHENTIC MANHOOD
YOUR STRATEGIC MOVE

RESOURCES ON THE FOLLOWING PAGES

A NOTE TO
HUSBANDS

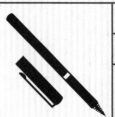

An Excerpt from Restless: Because You Were Made for More

Written by Zac Allen

It was a perfect, eighty-degree day on the lawn of a plantation house in downtown Little Rock.

This was the day all of our dreams would become a reality. I stood looking in Jennie's eyes, and before God, I promised to lead her by daily dying to my selfish desires, just as Christ did. The record states that the pastor read that day from Ephesians 5:28-30: "Husbands ought to love their wives as their own bodies. ... After all, no one ever hated their own body, but they feed and care for their body, just as Christ does the church—for we are members of his body" (NIV).

But honestly, I don't remember the ceremony very well or the charge of the pastor, or the vows I spoke to Jennie. I just know in the midst of sixteen years of marriage, many moves, four kids, mortgages, and unfulfilling jobs, the dreams we dreamed on many dates before marriage quickly gave way to a lot of weighty responsibility.

I went from trying to win this girl's heart and longing for her freedom to pursue God's dreams for her, to actually using the Bible's language of submission to kill any dream that would inconvenience or threaten me. So, not long after the wedding day, Jennie found herself with a passive-aggressive, emotionless husband, and her God-given passions and dreams began to die.

At the time, I thought I was right and biblically justified in my "leadership" of Jennie. But I was wrong. I had memorized "Wives, submit yourselves to your own husbands" but had no clue of what it meant for husbands to nourish and cherish their wives (Eph. 5:22 NIV).

Honestly, it took years for me to grow in maturity to see my error. And if you find yourself reading this and realizing you no longer have a clue how to nourish and cherish, take courage; neither do countless other men reading this-that their wives asked them to read. So hang with me because I want to help you lead your wives. My goal is not to beat you down, but rather to call you to one of the most noble callings of your life.

Husbands, to nourish and cherish your wife means to unleash your wife to be everything she has been designed to be in Christ.

Yes, that means you are to live with her in an understanding way: to know the hurts she brings into marriage, to know her passions, and to listen to her dreams, even when you have no clue what to do with them. To nourish and to cherish means you become the most powerful earthly display of unconditional love. And part of that unconditional love is shown as she gives herself to the many seemingly mediocre tasks of daily life.

② **I was insecure in who I was in Christ.** If I was not performing well at work or if I didn't have a fulfilling job, I felt like a failure. My worth was not coming from the approval of the God of the universe, but from the disapproval I felt internally. Here is what I know to be true: an insecure husband will never be able to cheer for his wife's calling or cherish and nourish her gifts.

BUT HUSBANDS, DON'T MISS THIS: TO NOURISH AND CHERISH ALSO MEANS TAKING THE INITIATIVE TO SHEPHERD HER GIFTS AND CALLINGS AND TO HELP HER DREAM.

So how did I miss all that? Why did the dreaming die so quickly after "I do"? I think I can boil down my failures to nourish and cherish to two reasons:

① **I had a darkened, jaded view of submission.** I used submission to squelch my wife so I could justify my "more important" pursuits. Of course few of us would say that as men, our callings and gifts and passions are more important than those of our wives. But that is often how I led. So tonight, or on a date this week, ask your wife if she feels safe to dream with you. Ask her if she feels cherished and empowered to use her gifts.

Insecure husbands think about themselves first. There were countless times early in my marriage when I would secretly resent my wife's gifts. Or maybe I would even be so noble to encourage her to use her gift of teaching, only to resent being left with the kids as she went to use those gifts.

It took me years to realize the problem wasn't being married to a passionate, gifted, "unsubmissive" wife who would start using her gifts only to have me reel her back into reality. The problem was me: my misunderstanding of my role to lead us as a team on mission, and my resentment of seeing my wife walking in freedom while I was immersed in my own insecurities.

So, husbands, if you are still reading this, I believe you really want your wife to be all she is designed to be in Christ. You want your children to see a mom serving and using her gifts in and outside your home. And I believe you want to want to sit across from your wife on that date and affirm her God-given dreams and callings.

This excerpt is from Jennie Allen, *Restless: Because You Were Made for More* (Nashville: W Publishing, 2013) and was used with the permission of the publisher.

DISCUSSION GUIDE

FOR EXPERIENCIN

"A MAN AND HIS MARRIAG

WITH YOUR WIFI

SESSION ONE: FOUNDATION

1. Of the three types of marriage discussed in this session (top-down, identical, and side-by-side), which best describes your marriage? Why?

2. Share with each other what it looks like for you (husband) to live out headship in your marriage.

3. Likewise, share with each other what it looks like for you (wife) to live out submission in your marriage.

PRAYER: Pray for each other that you will rely on God's grace toward each other as you live out your designed roles.

SESSION TWO: DIE TO LIVE

1. Identify your own self-centeredness and share with each other where it can show up most naturally in your marriage. Where is it easiest for you to have a "me" mentality?

2. Discuss what it could look like for both of you to live out the "Paradox Principle" (Die to Live) in your marriage.

3. We discussed four main areas of servant leadership for the husband (spiritual, emotional, financial, and physical). Discuss together which one comes most naturall (husband) in your marriage. Likewise, talk about the area (husband) where you could use the most encouragement and support.

PRAYER: Pray together that you'll both live out the "Paradox Principle" (Die to Live).

SESSION THREE: FRIENDSHIP

1. Share with each other which of the five characteristics of friendship stand out as the strongest in your marriage. Talk about which ones could be strengthened and what that would look like.

2. Talk about the different ways you spend your time relating with each other (back-to-back, shoulder-to-shoulder, and face-to-face). What could you do to enhance those i your relationship?

PRAYER: Pray together that God will deepen your marriage friendship.

At the end of session six, Tierce challenges us to consider downloading the video sessions of this volume and to watch them again with our wife. This Discussion Guide will help you maximize that experience.

You can purchase downloads of individual sessions or the entire series for a few dollars at **AUTHENTICMANHOOD.COM**

SESSION FOUR: INTIMACY

1. Share with each other the one thing you heard in this session that was the most insightful about intimacy in marriage.

2. As openly and honestly as you can, with a spirit of grace toward each other, share one thing you heard today about sexual intimacy that you would like to see applied in your marriage. (Warning: this is not a time to be defensive but an opportunity to build trust).

PRAYER: Pray that God will connect your hearts emotionally and spiritually as you grow in physical intimacy.

SESSION FIVE: THREATS

1. Share with each other whether any of the threats are of particular concern to you as threats to your marriage.

2. Discuss how each of you responds to conflict. Are you a bottler or a fighter?.

3. Talk about what it can look like when both of you offer the same grace to each other that Jesus offers to us.

PRAYER: Pray that God will bless you with both oneness and a spirit of grace in your marriage.

SESSION SIX: GAME-CHANGERS

1. Ask your wife to discuss a game changer you're good at that has blessed her and made her feel loved.

2. Ask your wife to identify three or four game-changers that would bless her the most and that would speak directly to her heart.

PRAYER: Pray together that God will bless you (husband) with the desire and the grace to love and serve your wife in meaningful ways and you (wife) with the desire and the grace to offer the support and encouragement he needs.

40 YEARS OF MARRIAGE

LOOKING
B A C K

MY WIFE AND I JUST CELEBRATED OUR 40TH
ANNIVERSARY IN THE MOUNTAINS OF COLORADO
WITH OUR THREE ADULT CHILDREN, OUR SON-IN-LAW,
AND OUR DAUGHTER-IN-LAW.

DURING THE TRIP OUR KIDS SHARED SEVERAL
INTERESTING OBSERVATIONS REGARDING OUR MARRIAGE.
HERE ARE FOUR THINGS I'D LIKE TO PASS ON TO
HUSBANDS THAT I AM GLAD I DID
AND WISH I HAD DONE EVEN BETTER.

WRITTEN BY
RICK CALDWELL

1. **PRAY FOR AND WITH YOUR WIFE.**
Pausing before you leave each morning to give your wife a hug and pray a short prayer with her is time well spent.

2. **REALIZE THAT LITTLE THINGS CAN BE BIG.**
Remembering not to slam the door or not to leave your dirty clothes on the floor may seem like little things, but they communicate to your wife that you love her, are thinking about her, and do not take her for granted.

3. **PARENT AS A TEAM.**
Always work together in guiding and disciplining your kids. Discuss situations in private so you can present a unified front.

4. **MAKE MEMORIES.**
Be intentional about creating experiences and scheduling trips that can be reflected on and enjoyed for a lifetime. Sometimes these memories actually become legendary.

On the Meaning of Sex

By J. Budziszewski

Our society is obsessed with sex—and yet we don't understand it at all. Acclaimed philosopher J. Budziszewski remedies the problem in this wise, gracefully written book about the nature, meaning, and mysteries of sexuality. On the Meaning of Sex corrects the most prevalent errors about sex—particularly those of the sexual revolution, which by mistaking pleasure for a good in itself, has caused untold pain and suffering.

Date Your Wife

By Justin Buzzard

Most men don't know how to date their wives. They did it before, but they've forgotten how, or they're trying, but it just doesn't seem to be working. Justin Buzzard helps men relearn this all-important skill from a position of security in the gospel of grace.

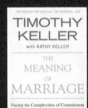

The Meaning of Marriage

By Timothy Keller

Modern culture would have you believe that everyone has a soul mate, that romance is the most important part of a successful marriage, that your spouse is there to help you realize your potential, that marriage does not mean forever but merely for now, and that starting over after a divorce is the best solution for seemingly intractable marriage issues. But these modern-day assumptions are wrong. Timothy Keller, with insights from Kathy, his wife of 37 years, shows marriage to be a glorious relationship that is also misunderstood and mysterious. The Meaning of Marriage offers instruction on how to have a successful marriage and is essential reading for anyone who wants to know God and love more deeply in this life.

The Masculine Mandate

By Richard D. Phillips

There is a crying need in the church today for men to be men. But competing visions for what a man is to be—some growing out of popular culture and others arising from flawed teaching in the church—are exacerbating the problem. Richard Phillips believes it is possible to cut through all this confusion by consulting the Bible. Only in the pages of Scripture, he asserts, can men find a clear explanation of their God-given roles as leaders, husbands, fathers, and churchmen.

What Is Marriage? Man and Woman: A Defense

By Sherif Girgis, Ryan T. Anderson, Robert P. George

Until yesterday no society had seen marriage as anything other than a conjugal partnership: a male-female union. What Is Marriage? identifies and defends the reasons for this historic consensus and shows why redefining civil marriage is unnecessary, unreasonable, and contrary to the common good.

The Seven Principles for Making Marriage Work

By John M. Gottman, Nan Silver

This book is the culmination of Gottman's life's work: the seven principles that guide couples on the path toward a harmonious and long-lasting relationship. Straightforward in their approach yet profound in their effect, these principles teach partners new and startling strategies for making their marriage work. Gottman helps couples focus on each other, on paying attention to the small day-to-day moments that, strung together, make up the heart and soul of any relationship. Being thoughtful about ordinary matters provides spouses with a solid foundation for resolving conflict when it does occur and for finding strategies to live with those issues that cannot be resolved.

A Severe Mercy

By Sheldon Vanauken

Beloved, profoundly moving account of th author's marriage, the couple's search fo faith and friendship with C. S. Lewis, and spiritual strength that sustained Vanauk after his wife's untimely death.

RESOURCES

SACRED MARRIAGE: WHAT IF GOD DESIGNED MARRIAGE TO MAKE US HOLY MORE THAN TO MAKE US HAPPY? BY GARY THOMAS

Everything about your marriage—everything—is filled with prophetic potential, with the capacity for discovering and revealing Christ's character. The respect you accord your partner; the forgiveness you humbly seek and graciously extend; the ecstasy, awe, and sheer fun of lovemaking; the history you and your spouse build with one another—in these and other facets of your marriage, Sacred Marriage uncovers the mystery of God's overarching purpose. This book may very well profoundly alter the contours of your marriage. It will most certainly change you.

THIS MOMENTARY MARRIAGE: A PARABLE OF PERMANENCE

BY JOHN PIPER

Though personal selfishness and cultural bondage obstruct the wonder of God's purpose, it is found in God's Word, where His design can awaken a glorious vision capable of freeing every person from small, Christ-ignoring, romance-intoxicated views. As Piper explains in reflecting on 40 years of matrimony, "Most foundationally, marriage is the doing of God. And ultimately, marriage is the display of God. It displays the covenant-keeping love between Christ and his people to the world in a way that no other event or institution does. Marriage, therefore, is not mainly about being in love. It's mainly about telling the truth with our lives. And staying married is not about staying in love. It is about keeping covenant and putting the glory of Christ's covenant-keeping love on display."

SEXUAL INTIMACY IN MARRIAGE

BY WILLIAM CUTRER

Every couple has those questions they don't know how or whom to ask! Sexual Intimacy in Marriage discusses the basics, like the definition of marriage, and the not-so-basic topics, such as achieving sexual pleasure and biblically OK sexual activity. This highly acclaimed, medically and biblically accurate book covers all the bases about sex in marriage with a sensitivity and frankness that every couple will appreciate.

HIS NEEDS, HER NEEDS: BUILDING AN AFFAIR-PROOF MARRIAGE

BY WILLARD F. HARLEY JR.

What will it take to make your marriage sizzle? Time after time, His Needs, Her Needs has topped the charts as the best marriage book available. More than any other, it has helped husbands and wives give each other what they need most in marriage.

THE GOOD GIRL'S GUIDE TO GREAT SEX

BY SHEILA WRAY GREGOIRE

Do bad girls really have more fun? Surveys say no. The women who are most likely to enjoy sex are married and religious. In other words, they're good girls! But good girls know that making sex great isn't about acting trashy. It's about recognizing what God really designed sex for and then learning how to reap all these benefits and joyfully enjoy your husband. Frank and contemporary, The Good Girl's Guide to Great Sex will give newly engaged and new brides—and some veteran wives—a Christian resource to answer their most intimate—and embarrassing—questions. In a conversational style, with lots of humorous anecdotes, the book will show that sex isn't just physical: it's also an emotional and spiritual experience. And we'll learn why commitment in a Christian marriage is the perfect recipe for a sex life that is out of this world!

CHECK OUT OTHER VOLUMES OF

33 THE SERIES™

Volume 1
A Man and His Design

Volume 2
A Man and His Story

Volume 3
A Man and His Traps

Volume 5
A Man and His Work

Volume 5
A Man and His Marriage

Volume 6
A Man and His Family

Purchase Individual Sessions and Entire Volumes at
authenticmanhood.com

SCRIPTURE REFERENCES

Proverbs 27:9 (ESV) "The sweetness of a friend comes from his earnest counsel."

Proverbs 27:17 (ESV) "Iron sharpens iron, and one man sharpens another."

Ephesians 5:28 (ESV) "Husbands should love their wives as their own bodies. He who loves his wife loves himself."

SUPPORTING RESOURCES

Buzzard, Justin. *Date Your Wife*. Wheaton, IL: Crossway, 2012. In this highly readable and short book, Buzzard provides husbands with very practical ideas for how to love, serve, and date their wives.

Blanchard, Ken, and Phil Hodges. *Lead like Jesus.* Nashville: Thomas Nelson, 2005. Blanchard and Hodges examine the life of Jesus and how He provided us with the perfect example of servant leadership.

The content in the previous resources does not necessarily reflect the opinion of Authentic Manhood. Readers should utilize these resources but form their own opinions.

ACTION PLAN

YOUR STRATEGIC MOVE | SESSION ONE : **FOUNDATION**

_____

_____

YOUR STRATEGIC MOVE | SESSION TWO : **DIE TO LIVE**

_____

_____

YOUR STRATEGIC MOVE | SESSION THREE : **FRIENDSHIP**

_____

_____

YOUR STRATEGIC MOVE | SESSION FOUR : **INTIMACY**

_____

_____

YOUR STRATEGIC MOVE | SESSION FIVE : **THREATS**

_____

_____

YOUR STRATEGIC MOVE | SESSION SIX : **GAME-CHANGERS**

_____

_____

A Man and His Marriage: Answer Key

SESSION ONE: FOUNDATION

I. 1. stuck
    2. momentary happiness
II. 2.
    - God's
    - alone
    - helper
    - cling
      ° temporary
III. 1.
    - top-down
    - identical
    - side-by-side
    3. servant leadership
    - servant
      ° grace
    4.
    - yes

SESSION TWO: DIE TO LIVE

I. 1. you

II. 1. happiness
    4. you
III. 1. die
    2. example, motivation
    - empowered
    3. healthy

IV.
    1.
    - superstar
    2.
    - emotions
    - feeling
    - fun

3.
- duty
- future
4.
- consuming

SESSION THREE: FRIENDSHIP

I. 1. friendship
    4. passivity
II. 1. together
    - intentionally
    - shared
    2. curiosity
    - student
    - growing
    3. trust
    - shared
    - best
    4.
    - reality
    - fix
    5.
    - common
III.
    1.
    - different
    - separate
    2.
    - alongside
    - communication
    3.
    - directly
    - your

SESSION FOUR: INTIMACY

I.   1.
    • *underemphasize*
    • *overemphasize*
    2.
        1. *biblical*
II.   2. *good*
    3. *enjoy*
        • *body*
    4.
        • *physical*
        • *worship*
III.
    1.
        • *season*
        • *manage*
        • *physical*
            ° *designed*
    2.
        i. *serve*
        ii. *Reassure*
        iii. *arousal*
        iv.
            • *comfortable*
        vi. *knowledge*
        vii. *roadblocks*

SESSION FIVE: THREATS

I.   1. *aware*
II.
    1.
        • *designed*

            ° *flee*
            ° *grace*
            •
            ° *commitment*

° *purity*

° *happiness*

• *grace*

° *trusts*

2.
    • *corrode*

    ° *avoid*

3.
    • *Disagreements*
    • *discuss*

5.
    • *meaning*
    • *savior*

SESSION SIX: GAME-CHANGERS

I.   1. *game-changers*
II.   1. *envisioning*
    2. *leadership*
    3. *imperfections*
    4. *fairly*
    5. *consultation*
    6. *follows through*
    7. *seasons*
    8. *distractions*
    9. *plan*
    10. *family*
    11. *small group*
    12. *schedule*
    13. *praises*
    14. *grow*
    15. *specifically*
    16. *Jesus*
    17. *influence*
    18. *traditions*
    19. *tough, tender*
    20. *grace*